THE HEINEMANN FIRST THESAURUS

HEINEMANN

For Jeremy and Joanne

First published by Macmillan Education Ltd 1987
Reprinted 1990 by Heinemann Children's Reference,
a division of Heinemann Educational Books Ltd,
Halley Court, Jordan Hill, Oxford OX2 8EJ
Companies and representatives throughout the world

Printed in Hong Kong

British Library Cataloguing in Publication Data

Pemberton, Gordon
The Heinemann first thesaurus: find your words here
1. English language — Synonyms
I. Title
423'.1 PE1591

ISBN 0 431 00080 8

contents

To parents and teachers	iv
How to use this book	v
Contents of the thesaurus	vii
Thesaurus	1
Index	71

To parents and teachers

This thesaurus is a collection of word lists relating to topics which children are likely to need in their written work.

Within their sections, the words are arranged by association of ideas rather than alphabetically. This is intended to give children additional help and to stimulate their thoughts on the topics about which they are writing.

The general vocabulary includes words which would not normally be found in children's vocabulary lists but which children easily recognise, often use in conversation, and sometimes include in their writing. Examples are *aqualung, cassette, roustabout, prescription, scampi, turbulence, tachograph* and *wetsuit.*

Included also are words that children recognise and use mainly in their shortened form. Examples of such words are *hi-fi, soccer, vet, fridge* and *artic.*

The vocabulary of this book also includes about seven per cent of words which are on the periphery of many children's vocabularies. They hear their parents or other adults use these words in association with particular circumstances. Though the children may not understand these words fully, they know of their association. Words of this kind have been deliberately included. Examples are *consultant, flexible, fluorescent, sympathetic* and *emergency.*

Many of the sections in the thesaurus have simple cross-references to other sections, so that a child is always given the opportunity of finding the maximum number of words associated with the topic on which he or she is writing. For example, the word *doctor* (in the section on 'Work') is given a direct and simple cross-reference to the section on **health**, where words associated with a doctor's duties are given. Similarly, the section on **indoor games** is cross-referenced with **toyshop**, and so on. There are approximately three hundred of these cross-references.

Important

When using this thesaurus a child will sometimes find a group of helpful words among which there is one word about whose meaning he or she is not sure. He or she should be encouraged to look up this word in a dictionary.

How to use this book

This book can be used in two ways to find the word you want.

The first way

To find a word that you have forgotten (it may be on the tip of your tongue!), look at the Contents pages. Look through the headings and find the most suitable one. Under that heading, find the section which seems likely to contain words on the subject you are writing about. Note its section number. Find that section in the main part of the book. In that section you will find the word you want, or a word like it.

For example, suppose that you have already used the word *annoyed* but you now want another word which means almost the same. Find *annoyed* in the index. You will see that the word *annoyed* has the section number 52 after it. Find section 52 in the main part of the book. There you will find other words which have meanings similar to the word *annoyed*, such as *displeased.*

The second way

Sometimes when you are writing, you need to use a word very similar to one you have already used. You do not want to repeat the word you have used, but you cannot think of another one like it.

This time look in the index at the end of the book. Find the word you have already used. It will have a section number after it. Find that section in the main part of the book and it will contain other words which have similar meanings.

For example, suppose that you have already used the word **annoyed** but you now want another word which means almost the same. Find **annoyed** in the index. You will see that the word **annoyed** has the section number 52 after it.

Find section 52 in the main part of the book. There you will find other words which have meanings similar to the word **annoyed**, such as **displeased**.

Important

If you see a word that you would like to use, but you are not quite sure of its real meaning, *look it up in your dictionary*.

Contents of the thesaurus with section numbers

personal
family 1
relatives 2
birth 3
marriage 4
death 5
friends 6

home
house (outside) 7
house (inside) 8
downstairs 9
kitchen 10
utensils 11
bedroom 12
bathroom 13
loft 14
garden 15

school
building 16
adults 17
classroom 18
class 19
educational aids 20

school subjects
English 21
mathematics 22
science 23
history 24
historical periods 25
geography 26
art 27
craft 28
needlework 29
physical education 30
music 31

health
general 32
disease 33
accident 34
doctor 35
dentist 36
body 37
organs 38
bones 39
positions 40
movements (slow) 41
movements (fast) 42

senses
sight (bright) 43
sight (dull) 44
hearing (loud) 45
hearing (quiet) 46
smell 47
touch 48
taste 49

feelings
pleasure 50
sadness 51
anger 52
fear 53
courage 54
excitement 55
interest 56
boredom 57

clothing
outer 58
trunk and legs 59
feet 60
underwear 61
head 62
neck 63
fasteners 64
babywear 65
materials 66

people
build 67
complexion 68
hair 69
character 70
appearance 71

work
milk 72
post 73
coal 74
refuse 75
police 76
fire 77
ambulance 78
doctor 79
dentist 80
nurse 81
chemist 82
vet 83

Contents of the thesaurus with section numbers

shop 84
newsagent 85
buses 86
trucks 87
trains 88
joiner 89
surveyor 90
architect 91
building 92
bricklayer 93
plumber 94
painter 95
decorator 96
electrician 97
mechanic 98
gas fitter 99
teacher 100
head teacher 101
cook 102
caretaker 103
cleaner 104
editor 105
printer 106
lawyer 107
judge 108
engineer 109
military 110
docks 111
shipbuilder 112
steelworker 113
miner 114
car worker 115
fisherman 116
seaman 117
oil driller 118
hairdresser 119
model 120
dressmaker 121
secretary 122
waitress 123
accountant 124
computer programmer 125
librarian 126
farming 127
shepherd 128
labourer 129
apprentice 130

power
electricity 131
oil 132
coal 133
gas 134
nuclear power 135

tools
bench 136
domestic 137
garden 138
electronics 139
computer 140
cooking 141
farm 142

food
nutrition 143
meals 144
vegetables 145
fruit 146
cereals 147
meat 148
fish 149
groceries 150
beverages 151
cooking 152
confectionery 153
café 154

shops
dairy 155
baker 156
grocery 157
butcher 158
sweetshop 159
toyshop 160
post office 161
chemist 162
supermarket 163
furniture 164
ironmonger 165
florist 166
electrics 167
hi-fi 168
television 169
tobacconist 170
department store 171
card shop 172
hairdresser 173
clothing (men's) 174
clothing (women's) 175
wine store 176

Contents of the thesaurus with section numbers

shopping
shops 177
market 178
delivery 179
purchasing 180
price 181
carrying 182

recreation
play 183
park 184
indoors 185
outdoors 186
television 187
hi-fi 188
theatre 189
concert 190
cinema 191
circus 192
fair 193
books 194

sport
general 195
football 196
rugby football 197
cricket 198
hockey 199
athletics 200
netball 201
rounders 202
swimming 203
tennis 204
table tennis 205
show jumping 206
motor racing 207
cycle racing 208
fishing 209
golf 210
boxing 211
wrestling 212
snooker 213

environment
universe 214
planet Earth 215
rock 216
minerals 217
country 218
town 219
seaside 220
underwater 221
farm 222
mountain 223
river 224
park 225
buildings 226

transport
road 227
motorway 228
features 229
repairs 230
vehicle 231
parts 232
garage 233
bus 234
truck 235
motorbike 236
animal transport 237
pedestrian 238
rail 239
railway journey 240
locomotive 241
rolling stock 242
water transport 243
ship 244
yacht 245
crew 246
port 247
sea 248
canal 249
airline 250
airport 251
route 252
altitude 253
balloon 254
space transport 255
astronaut 256
lunar expedition 257

nature
weather 258
meteorology 259
temperature 260
pets 261
domestic animals 262
wild creatures (Britain) 263
wild creatures (overseas) 264

Contents of the thesaurus with section numbers

birds (Britain) 265
birds (overseas) 266
water creatures 267
invertebrates 268
reptiles 269
trees 270
gardens 271
air 272
water 273
rain 274
mist 275
wet 276
waterworks 277
domestic water 278
fire 279

time
measurement 280
seasons 281
calendar 282
days 283
daytime 284
the clock 285
when? 286
how often? 287
how soon? 288

communications
language 289
television 290
radio 291
telephone 292
letters 293
newspaper 294

law
law-making 295
police 296
court 297
punishment 298
crime 299

basic descriptions
size (small) 300
size (large) 301
shape (regular) 302
shape (irregular) 303
colour 304
dark 305
light 306
red 307
blue 308
green 309
yellow 310
brown 311
purple 312
textures 313

THESAURUS

personal

1

family
mother
father
parents
single parent
husband
wife
brother
half-brother
sister
half-sister
twins
son
step-son
daughter
step-daughter
grandparents
grandmother
grandfather
grandchild
granddaughter
grandson
ancestor
descendant

2

relatives
uncle
aunt
nephew
niece
cousin

relation
brother-in-law
sister-in-law
mother-in-law
father-in-law

3

birth
baby
born
birthday

4

marriage
bachelor
spinster
engaged
ring
married
wedding
bride
bridegroom
bridesmaid
best man
church
service
registry office
reception
party
invitation
guests
honeymoon
separated
divorced

5

death
died
funeral
buried
cemetery
cremated
crematorium

6

friends
friendship
best friend
playmate
partner
companion
mate
comrade
team-mate
helper
supporter
neighbour

home

7

house (outside)

detached
semi-detached
terrace
bungalow
flat
apartment
cottage
caravan
mobile home
veranda
conservatory
porch
garage
coalplace
path
pavement
wall
fence
hedge
gate
roof
slates
tiles
thatch
chimney
TV aerial
gutter
fall-pipe
downspout
drain
yard
patio
stone
brick
window
double-glazed
french window
patio door
entrance
door
doorstep
knocker
knob
ring
letter box

8

house (inside)

carpet
rug
mat
lino
tiles
skirting board
light
lamp
switch
curtains
net
blind
decoration
wallpaper
radiator

9

downstairs
hall
cloakroom
utility room
lobby
passage
coat-hook
mirror
stairs
banisters
handrail
dining-room
table
chairs
tablecloth
place-mats
sideboard
trolley
sitting-room
lounge
armchair
easy-chair
settee
couch
sofa
divan
three-piece suite
cushion
bookcase
cabinet
china
glass
shelf
shelves
ornament
vase
clock
hearth
fireplace
grate
mantlepiece
fender
poker
tongs
coal scuttle
gas fire
electric fire
picture
photograph
piano
television
radio
video
stereo
music centre
home computer
telephone
[see 164, 168, 290, 291]

10

kitchen
fitted kitchen
cooker
hob
electric
gas
stove
oven
microwave
grill
hotplate
burner
refrigerator
fridge
freezer
dishwasher
washing-machine
tumble-drier
sink
unit
waste-disposal unit
tap
mixer tap
drainer
cupboard
stool
worktop
work surface
scullery
pantry
larder
boiler
oil
solid fuel
central heating
thermostat
radiators

11

utensils
pans
pots
kettle
cutlery
crockery
dishes

contd.

tray
toaster
blender
food processor
grinder
bread
cutting board

12
bedroom
single bed
double bed
mattress
blanket
sheet
duvet
continental quilt
eiderdown
bedspread
pillow
bolster
cot
bunks
dressing-table
mirror
wardrobe
chest of drawers
tallboy
[see 164]

13
bathroom
bath
bathmat
shower
washbasin
toilet
bidet
mirror
nailbrush
facecloth
soap
toothbrush
toothpaste
glass
shampoo
bubble bath
towels
airing cupboard
loofah
sponge
brush
seat
flush
paper

14
loft
attic
storage
water tank
cistern
immersion heater
pipes
lagging
fibreglass
insulation

15
garden
soil
earth
plant
flower
shrub
vegetable
grass
lawn
sandpit
swing
paddling pool
washing-line
weeds
manure
peat
compost heap
fertiliser
toolshed
lean-to
lawnmower
hovermower
spade
fork
rake
hoe
cold frame
greenhouse
watering-can
hosepipe
spray
wheelbarrow
[see 138, 271]

school

16

building
entrance
steps
playground
hall
classroom
staffroom
school office
head's room
corridor
stairs
library
music room
kitchen
dining-room
boiler-house
swimming pool
playing field
garden
hut
[see 100-104]

17

adults
head teacher
headmistress
headmaster
deputy head
teacher
secretary
caretaker
cleaner
dinner lady
supervisor
cook
gardener
parents
[see 100-104]

18

classroom
blackboard
chalk
duster
desk
lid
seat
chair
table
cupboard
shelf
rack
clock
bookcase
sink
tap
cloth
books
pen
ink
pencil
biro
crayon
rubber
ruler

19

class
form
group
team
register
reading

contd.

writing
copy
lesson
period
break
timetable
bell
term
holiday
children
pupils
older
younger

20

educational aids
television
video recorder
radio
tape recorder
cassette recorder
record-player
wall map
wall chart
globe
picture
illustration
textbook
exercise book
[see 100]

school subjects

21

English
story
play
poem
composition
essay
exercise
question
answer
spelling
dictation
grammar
punctuation
sentence
phrase
clause
word
comma
full stop
capital letter
paragraph
work
mark
test
examination
report

22

mathematics
arithmetic
sums
add
subtract
multiply
divide
numbers
figures
fractions
decimals

calculate
calculator
computer
tables
ruler
shape
square
circle
rectangle
triangle
measurement
estimate
graph
metre
centimetre
litre
gram
kilogram
kilometre
tonne

23

science
experiment
test
apparatus
observe
measure
result
magnet
lens
magnifier
thermometer
burner
battery
scientist

24

history
time
past
old
ancient
prehistoric
date
event
battle
king
queen
prince
crusade
coat-of-arms
armour
chain-mail
helmet
horse
castle
defend
siege
dungeon
serf
conquer
civil war
parliament
republic

25

historical periods
prehistoric
Roman
Saxon
Dark Ages
Norman
Plantagenet
Tudor
Stuart
Hanoverian
Victorian
Edwardian
modern

26

geography
atlas
map
scale
chart
globe
country
capital
island
sea
ocean
coast
north
south
east
west
pole
equator
hill
mountain
river
lake
channel
canal
seaport

contd.

products
raw materials
industries
transport
[see 215]

27

art
brush
paint
paper
water
colour
pencil
draw
sketch
scene
sculpture
pattern
collage
mobile
crayon
pastel
shadow

28

craft
clay
Plasticine
paper
cardboard
balsa wood
string
scissors
knife
fold
crease
bend
score
cut
stick
paste
glue
model
design

29

needlework
knitting
needles
pins
wool
woollen
cast on
cast off
purl
plain
rib
material
thread
sew
sewing-machine
stitch
tack
hem
seam
embroider

30

physical education
P.E.
dance
run
chase
hop
jump
vault
handstand
cartwheel
somersault
astride
climb
wall bars
vest
shorts
pumps
plimsolls
rope
ball
catch
game
playing field
pitch
court
team

31

music
singing
piano
pianist
voice
solo

choir
recorder
play
violin
guitar
amplifier
notes
concert
instrument
sheet music
band
orchestra

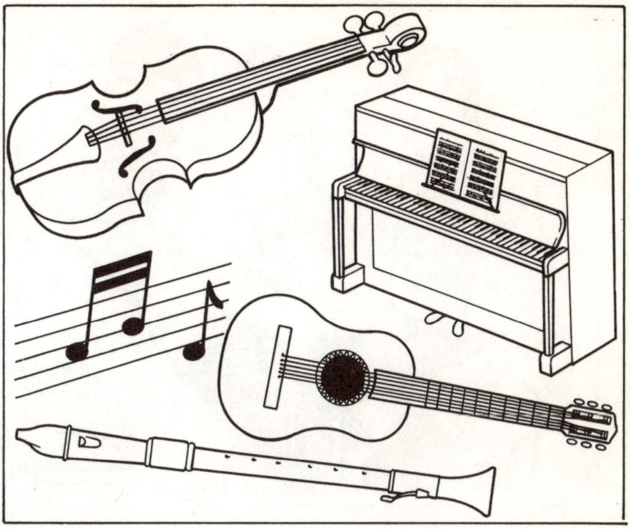

health

32

general
healthy
fit
well
vigorous
robust
strong
unhealthy
ill
sick
unwell
feverish
ailing
feeble
frail
delicate
check-up
diet
[see 67]

33

disease
illness
germ
virus
epidemic
antibiotics
disinfectant
septic
antiseptic
temperature
thermometer
injection
immunise
vaccination
needle
stomach-ache
cough
cold
flu
influenza
tonsilitis
mumps
measles
chicken pox
bronchitis
whooping cough
asthma
hay fever

34

accident
ambulance
stretcher
police
oxygen
kiss of life
broken
fracture
X-ray
operation
theatre
surgeon
anaesthetic
unconscious

contd.

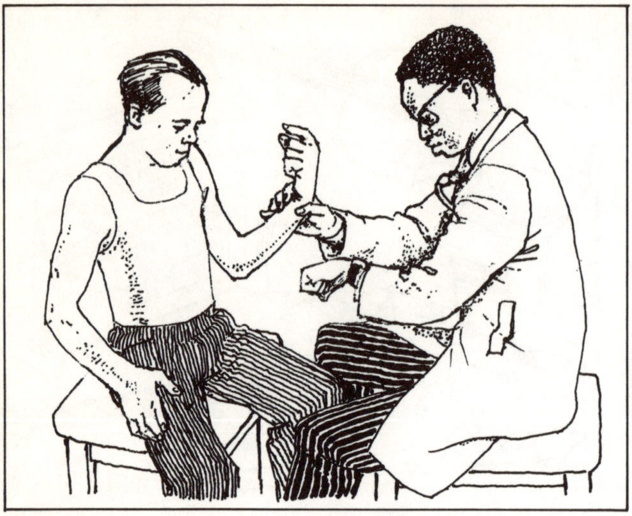

hospital
ward
nurse
patient
bandage
plaster cast
visitor
convalescent
[see 81]

35

doctor
surgery
waiting-room
stethoscope
specialist
consultant
clinic
blood-test
treatment
injection
prescription
chemist

medicine
ointment
pills
tablets
lotion
[see 78-82]

36

dentist
dental surgeon
surgery
chair
couch
teeth
gums
molars
examine
injection
numb
filling
drill
extraction
[see 80]

37

body
head
scalp
hair
forehead
temple
face
ear
eye
eyelid
eyelash
pupil
iris
lens
retina
nose
nostril
cheek
mouth
lip
tongue
teeth
neck
trunk
shoulder
chest
arm
leg
joint
elbow
knee
wrist
ankle
hand
thumb

finger
nail
knuckle
palm
foot
instep
toe
muscle

38
organs

lung
heart
beat
blood
artery
vein
stomach
liver
kidney
intestine
digestion

39
bones

skeleton
skull
jaw
collar-bone
shoulder-blade
rib
breast-bone
ribcage
backbone
spine
vertebrae
disc
hip
pelvis
thigh-bone
shin-bone
kneecap

40
positions

stand
sit
lie
lean
sprawl
recline
squat
lounge

41
movements (slow)

linger
loiter
dawdle
crawl
creep
toddle
waddle
amble
hobble
hop
limp
saunter
plod
shuffle
shamble
slither
stagger
lurch
stumble
totter
topple
trudge
stroll

42
movements (fast)

stride
march
trot
run
hurry
scurry
scamper
charge
rush
hurtle
sprint
chase
skip
dance
romp
dart
caper
jump
leap
spring
fall

senses

43
sight (bright)
blinding
brilliant
shiny
clear
visible
readable
transparent
glossy
gleaming
reflection
alight
ablaze
luminous
radiant
glowing
fluorescent
glaring
sparkling
glittering
dazzling
flashing
twinkling

44
sight (dull)
faint
opaque
dim
misty
cloudy
foggy
blurred
shady
unlit
dark
indistinct
unreadable
invisible

45
hearing (loud)
ear-splitting
deafening
noise
roar
bang
crash
explosion
thunder
boom
echo
din
rumble
clang
slam
clash
ring
clamour
clatter
resound
uproar
creak
crunch
splash

46
hearing (quiet)
peaceful
tranquil
lull
hushed
faint
dumb
mute
inaudible
soundless
soundproof
noiseless
silence

47
smell
odour
aroma
tang
smelly
foul
stuffy
stink
stench
reek
rank
musty
offensive
overpowering
suffocating
acrid
fetid
pungent
clean

fragrant
fragrance
fresh
perfume
sweet
scented

48

touch
soft
downy
velvety
smooth
polished
glossy
slippery
flexible
pliable
flabby
springy
hairy
clammy
greasy
oily
sticky
slimy
wet
hard
firm
solid
rough
coarse
uneven
jagged
wrinkled

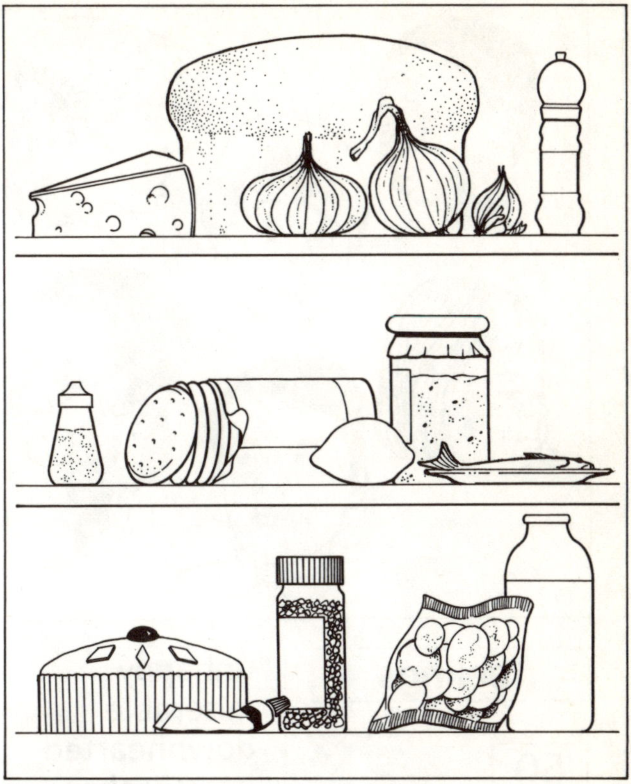

sharp
brittle
crumbling
prickly
lumpy
thick
thin

49

taste
tasty
sweet
rich
sickly
sour
acid
sharp
salty
savoury
hot
stale
tasteless
bland
insipid
luscious
spicy
tart
bitter
strong
mild
delicious
appetising
palatable

feelings

50

pleasure
pleased
happy
glad
excited
joyful
delighted
satisfied
contented
cheerful
gratified

51

sadness
sad
sorry
unhappy
miserable
downhearted
heartbroken
dismal
downcast
discouraged
distressed
mournful
sorrowful
gloomy
dejected
depressed
grief-stricken

52

anger
cross
fed-up
angry
annoyed
furious
vexed
displeased
irritated
discontented

53

fear
afraid
frightened
scared
terrified
fearful
worried
horrified
anxious
uneasy
timid
cowardly

54

courage
brave
bold
daring
plucky
adventurous
fearless
valiant
courageous
heroic
cool

55
excitement
excited
eager
thrilled
enthusiastic
elated
aroused
inspired
turned-on

56
interest
interested
curious
fascinated
attracted
attentive
gripped
captivated
sympathetic

57
boredom
bored
tired
weary
listless
uninterested
lackadaisical

clothing

58
outer
coat
overcoat
anorak
cagoule
duffel coat
wind-cheater
mackintosh
raincoat
gloves
mittens
legwarmers
suit
jacket
blazer
tunic
waistcoat
pocket
overalls

59
trunk and legs
shirt
sleeve
cuff
T-shirt
blouse
sweater
pullover
jumper
jersey
cardigan
dress
gown
skirt
kilt
smock
swimsuit
trunks
bikini
trousers
jeans
denims
dungarees
shorts
belt
buckle
braces
socks
stockings
tights

60
feet
pair
shoes
boots
wellingtons
pumps
plimsolls
sandals
trainers
slippers

61
underwear
vest
singlet
pants
knickers
briefs
bra
nightdress
pyjamas
dressing gown
housecoat

62
head
hat
cap
beret
hood
turban

63
neck
scarf
collar
shawl
muffler
tie
tie-pin
bow-tie
cravat

64
fasteners
button
buttonhole
zip fastener
Velcro
press-stud
hook and eye
laces
ribbon
brooch
clasp
clip
toggle

65
babywear
nappy
shawl
baby-gro
bonnet
bootees
mittens
matinee coat

66
materials
cotton
wool
tweed
velvet
cord
silk
nylon
Terylene
Crimplene
polyester

people

67
build
tall
lanky
short
small
fat
plump
lean
thin
slim
slender
sturdy
thickset
brawny
muscular
powerful
robust
strong
trim
dainty
tiny
puny
frail
delicate
gaunt
bent
disabled
deformed
[see 32]

68

complexion
pale
fair
freckles
dark
sallow
swarthy
bronzed
dusky
ruddy
tanned
sunburnt
wrinkled
weatherbeaten

69

hair
blond(e)
golden
fair
black
brown
mousey
auburn
grey
white
wavy
straight
curly
plaited
tousled
tangled
bald
beard

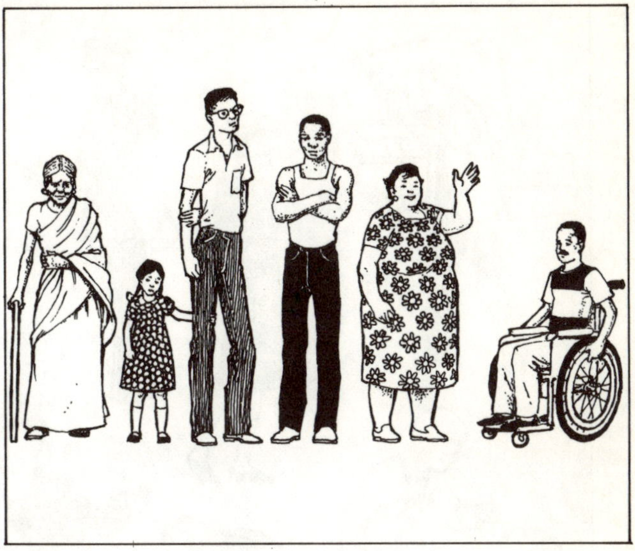

moustache
sideboards
sideburns
[see 119]

70

character
pleasant
charming
courteous
friendly
sympathetic
affectionate
cheerful
humorous
reliable
dependable
sincere
kind
gentle
loving
truthful
honest
fair
unselfish
shy
reserved
unpleasant
wicked
cruel
selfish
unkind
mean
sly
cunning
jealous
quarrelsome
ungrateful
stern
boastful
arrogant
proud
stubborn
deceitful
conceited

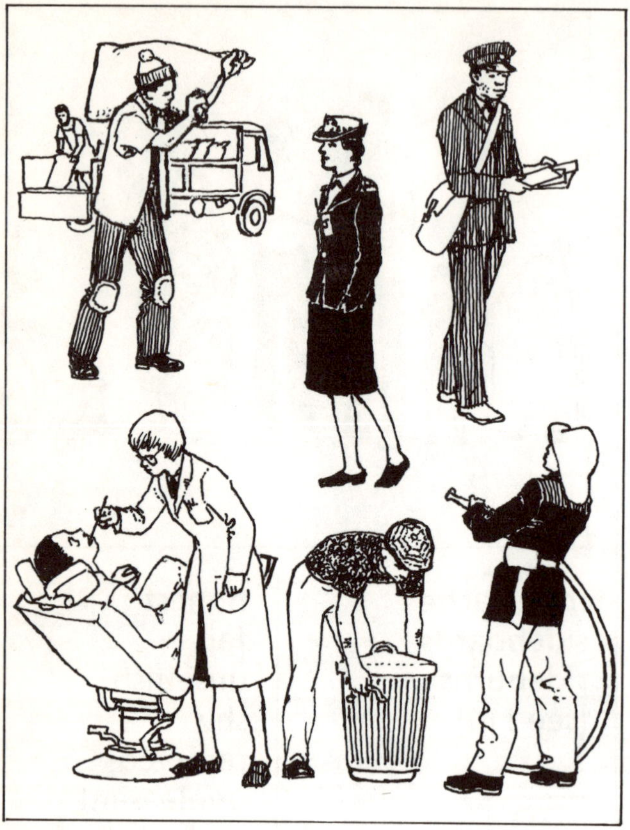

71

appearance
delightful
clean
fashionable
smart
neat
elegant
dull
drab
shabby
tattered
dirty
untidy
unkempt

work

72

milk
roundsman
delivery
dairy
cream
yogurt
bottle
carton
float
tanker
farm
[see 155]

73

post
post office
sorting office
letters
parcels
stamps
collection
delivery
postbox
pillar box
mail van
[see 161, 293]

74

coal
coalyard
coke
anthracite
smokeless fuel
sacks
scales
pit
colliery
winding gear
miner
[see 114, 133]

75

refuse
refuse truck
refuse tip
rubbish

bin
waste bin
bin bag
litter
dustman

76

police
policewoman
police station
sergeant
constable
inspector
detective
superintendent
uniform
helmet
whistle
radio
truncheon
beat
[see 296]

77

fire
fireman
fire-station
fire-engine
appliance
siren
helmet
axe
hose
hydrant
water
ladder
turntable
fireguard
fire-extinguisher
fire-blanket
[see 279]

78

ambulance
depot
driver
stretcher
first-aid
emergency
oxygen
flashers
siren
hospital
[see 34]

79

doctor
health centre
surgery
waiting room
examination
stethoscope
treatment
prescription
[see 35]

80

dentist
surgery
chair
couch
teeth
examine
injection
numb
drill
filling
extraction
[see 36]

81

nurse
clinic
hospital
matron
sister
staff nurse
midwife
district nurse
[see 34]

82

chemist
dispense
medicine
bandage
pills
tablets
ointment
bottles
jars

contd.

prescription
[see 162]

83

vet
veterinary surgeon
surgery
animals
pets
examination
treatment
operation
[see 261, 262]

84

shop
assistant
counter
goods
stock
display
service
self-service
till
money
[see 177-182]

85

newsagent
newspapers
magazines
sweets
cigarettes
tobacco

86

buses
driver
conductor
one-man bus
pay-as-you-enter
exact fare
route
bell
stop
ticket
token
[see 227]

87

trucks
lorry
van
load
route
destination
delivery
transport café
meal
rest
radio
tachograph
[see 227, 235]

88

trains
locomotive
coach
guard
journey
ticket-collector
controls
signals
station
unmanned station
level-crossing
siding
[see 239, 242]

89

joiner
carpenter
wood
beams
boards
frames
joints
saw
hammer
nails
screwdriver
screws
drill
[see 136]

90

surveyor
poles
sighting
theodolite
levels
measuring
measurement
plan
map

91

architect
architecture
office
drawing-board
perspective
drawing
plans
model
style
[see 226]

92

building
building site
foundations
walls
floor
roof
windows
double glazing
doors
stairs
path
[see 226]

93

bricklayer
mortar
trowel
spirit-level
stringline
conveyor
hod
[see 7, 226]

94

plumber
pipes
blowlamp
boiler
water tank
cistern
toilet
taps
overflow
freeze
burst
leak
flood
[see 7]

95

painter
brushes
scraper
blowlamp
primer
undercoat
gloss paint
non-drip
emulsion
ladder
[see 7]

96

decorator
wallpaper
paste
scissors
table
hang
plumbline
pattern
match
drybrush
[see 7]

97

electrician
electricity
circuit
switch
wires
connect
current
socket
plug
fuse
meter
shock
spark
[see 7, 167]

98

mechanic
spanner
wrench
drill
bolt
gauge
weld
blowtorch
[see 232, 233]

99

gas fitter
pipes
join
joint
leak
smell
repair
meter

100

teacher
class
children
blackboard
desk
books
marking
correction
help
homework
[see 16-32]

101

head teacher
headmistress
headmaster
office
interview
assembly
[see 16-32]

102

cook
kitchen
stoves
ovens
prepare

meals
roast
boil
grill
fry
[see 16]

103

caretaker
boiler-room
heating
fuel
oil
coke
keys
doors
locks
gate
windows
ladder
repairs
[see 16, 137]

104

cleaner
vacuum cleaner
brush
duster
cloth
mop
sponge
soap
water
disinfectant
[see 16, 137]

105

editor
publisher
journalist
reporter
news
newspaper
articles
magazines
books
edit
deadline
[see 294]

106

printer
paper
ink
type
colour
setting
proofs
machines
folding
cutting
[see 194, 294]

107

lawyer
office
clerk
brief
solicitor
client
case
documents
[see 297]

108

judge
magistrate
barrister
court
oath
defence
defendant
prosecution
witness
accused
prisoner
jury
verdict
innocent
guilty
sentence
appeal
prison
[see 297, 298]

109

engineer
mechanic
fitter
workshop
machines
bench
lathe
drill
cutter
[see 136]

110
military
soldier
sailor
airman
marine
war
fight
attack
defend

111
docks
docker
ship
ferry
car ferry
roll-on
roll-off
load
unload
cargo
container
crane
fork-lift truck
warehouse
[see 243, 247]

112
shipbuilder
shipyard
crane
gantry
slipway
keel
hull
steel
plates
rivets
launch
[see 243, 247]

113
steelworker
ore
coke
blast furnace
molten
metal
ingots
power hammer
forging
casting

114
miner
colliery
mine
pit
shaft
hard hat
cage
seam
coalface
conveyor belt
pithead
baths
dirt
danger
[see 74, 133]

115
car worker
assembly-line
car-bodies
welding
electrics
assembling
bolts
nuts
spanners
screws
screwdriver
multiple
hinges
fitting
testing
spraying
polishing
[see 231, 232]

116
fisherman
boat
nets
trawl
seas
shoal
catch
storm
oilskins
radar

port
docks
[see 243-248]

117

seaman
ship
deck
ropes
hold
cargo
winch
derrick
storm
oilskins
radar
port
harbour
docks
[see 243-248]

118

oil-driller
roustabout
oil rig
hard hat
drills
pipes
platform
helipad
gusher
on-stream
[see 132]

119

hairdresser
scissors
comb
shampoo
set
style
permanent-wave
tint
dye
drier
blow-drier
[see 69, 173]

120

model
clothes
background
pose
camera
photograph
lighting
magazines

121

dressmaker
tailor
cloth
scissors
tape measure
pattern
sewing-machine
fitting
pressing
[see 174, 175]

122

secretary
typist
clerk
office
desk
typewriter
shorthand
notebook
file
ledger
photocopier

123

waitress
uniform
table
cutlery
crockery
glassware
tablecloth
tray
menu
order
courses
bill
[see 144, 154]

124

accountant
cashier
accounts
budget
income
expenditure
balance
calculator
computer
tax

125

computer programmer
computer operator
program
software
hardware
disc
screen
print-out

126

librarian
lending library
catalogue
author
fiction
non-fiction
reference
shelves
borrowing
[see 194]

127

farming
farmhouse
fields
arable
poultry
crops
machinery
ploughing
reaping
harvest
[see 142, 222]

128

shepherd
sheep
sheepdog
flock
ram
ewe
lamb
shearing
wool
[see 222]

129

labourer
spade
shovel
pick
dig
excavate
[see 230]

130

apprentice
apprenticeship
learning
training
practice
practising
study
examinations
qualify

power

131

electricity
power station
generator
turbine
dynamo
cables
pylons
distribution
[see 167]

132

oil
rig
drill
pipe
tanker
refinery
lubricating
paraffin
petrol
diesel
kerosene
[see 118]

133

coal
coalmine
pithead
screens
grades
hoppers
railways
wagons
coal trains
docks
power station
coalyard
[see 74, 114]

134

gas
North Sea
pipeline
gasholder
heating
cooking

135

nuclear power
atomic energy
reactor
water-cooled
gas-cooled
uranium
plutonium
radiation
danger

tools

136

bench
hammer
screwdriver

contd.

saw
chisel
spanner
mallet
plane
vice
brace and bit
pliers
pincers
drill
file
soldering iron
nail
screw
bolt
nut
washer
electric tools
[see 89, 98, 165]

137

domestic
broom
brush
dustpan
vacuum cleaner
mop
bucket
floorcloth
duster
feather duster
chamois leather
[see 103, 104]

138

garden
spade
fork
rake
hoe
trowel
shears
secateurs
lawnmower
rotavator
hedge clipper
hosepipe
broom
wheelbarrow
watering-can
water-butt
[see 15, 271]

139

electronics
calculator
computer
program
word processor
print-out
photocopier

140

computer
terminal
interface
floppy disc
cassette
byte
pixel
database
hardware
software
program
[see 125]

141

cooking
knife
fork
spoon
slice
can-opener
bottle-opener
mixer
blender
food processor
toaster
kettle
whisk
sieve
scales
rolling-pin
colander
scissors
basin
jug
pot
[see 10, 102, 152, 153]

142

farm
tractor
harrow
plough
roller
seeder
mower
hay-whisk
binder
combine harvester
stacker
potato-digger
silo
[see 127, 218, 222]

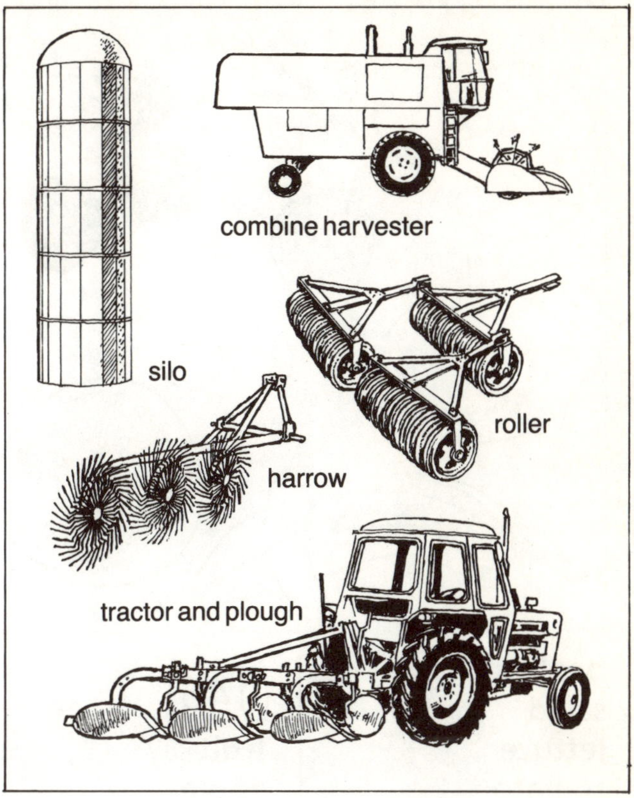

food

143

nutrition
minerals
fats
carbohydrates
vitamins
calories
trace elements
protein

144

meals
eating
eat
ate
drink
drank
breakfast
lunch
tea
high tea
dinner
supper
dishes
main course
pudding
sweet
dessert
snack
take-away
[see 10, 49, 102, 123, 152, 153, 154]

145

vegetables
potatoes
crisps
chips
yam
peas
beans
cabbage
cauliflower
carrot
mango
turnip
swede
okra
parsnip

contd.

beetroot
salad
lettuce
tomato
radish
cress
watercress
spinach
celery
cucumber
courgette
aubergine
sprouts
broccoli
leek
marrow
parsley
mint
garlic
sage
frozen vegetables

146

fruit
apple
pear
core
orange
satsuma
tangerine
peel
juicy
pips
banana
skin
lemon
pineapple
strawberry
raspberry
gooseberry
blackberry
currant
raisin
peach
apricot
plum
damson
prune
cherry
grape
melon
nectarine
tomato
avocado
kiwi fruit
peanut
hazel nut
walnut

147

cereals
wheat
oats
barley
rye
corn
corn flakes
rice
rice crispies
bran
sago
tapioca
spaghetti
macaroni
mealie flour
[see 156, 157]

148

meat
bacon
lamb
mutton
beef
pork
ham
chicken
turkey
veal
rabbit
liver
kidney
tongue
sausage
salami
hamburger
beefburger
mince
minced beef
steak
chop
[see 158]

149

fish
fingers
paste
cod
haddock
hake
plaice
herring
kipper
sardine
salmon
tuna
whiting
sole
mackerel
crab
shrimp
prawn
scampi
lobster
oyster
[see 116, 267]

150

groceries
bread
loaf
loaves
butter
margarine
milk
cream
cheese
egg
yogurt
sugar
jam
syrup
honey
fat
lard
cooking-oil
salt
pepper
mustard
sauce
pickles
vinegar
[see 157]

151

beverages
tea
cocoa
milk shake
coffee
fruit juice
squash
minerals
pop
coke
[see 157]

152

cooking
cooked
boiled
fried
fry
roast
grilled
baked
stewed
poached
scrambled
mashed
minced
toasted
sandwich
omelette

contd.

pastry
gravy
[see 10, 102, 123, 153, 154]

153

confectionery
pie
tart
flan
cake
bun
muffin
scone
crumpet
biscuit
sponge
custard
jelly
ice cream
[see 156]

154

café
tables
cutlery
crockery
menu
condiments
sauces
waitress
order
service
bill
tip
tray
cafeteria
self-service
[see 123]

shops

155

dairy
milk
cream
butter
cheese
yogurt
eggs
bottles
cartons
packs
[see 72]

156

baker
flour
yeast
bread
loaf
loaves
buns
pies
cakes
tarts
[see 147, 153]

157

grocery
dry goods
beverages
cereals
preserves
tins
jars
packets
bottles
[see 147, 151]

158

butcher
meat
beef
lamb
pork
bacon
ham
veal
chicken
turkey
liver
kidney
sausage
minced beef
meat pie
[see 148]

159

sweetshop
sweets
chocolates

bars
blocks
toffee
pastilles
chewing gum
packets
bags
tubes
boxes

160

toyshop
doll
soldier
model
car
painting set
train set
doll's house
easel
game
scrap book
puzzle
skipping rope
bricks
[see 185, 186]

161

post office
stamps
letters
parcels
air mail
weight
scales
pension
licence
savings bank
[see 73, 293]

162

chemist
prescription
medicine
pills
tablets
ointment
bandage
cosmetics
powder
perfume
baby food
toilet articles
films
[see 82]

163

supermarket
wire basket
trolley
shelves
frozen food
checkout
till

164

furniture
table
chair
stool
easy-chair
rocking-chair
cupboard
bed
bunk
wardrobe

contd.

chest of drawers
dressing-table
tallboy
suite
settee
sofa-bed
carpet
rug
mat
[see 9, 12]

165

ironmonger
tools
utensils
pots
pans
bins
nails
screws
[see 136, 137]

166

florist
flowers
bunches
sprays
bouquets
wreaths
plants
pots
vases

167

electrics
bulbs
batteries
wire
cable
plugs
fuses
switches
connectors
[see 97, 131]

168

hi-fi
high-fidelity
radio tuner
amplifier
record-player
disc
L.P.
album
single
sleeve
tape recorder
cassette deck
mono
stereo
compact disc
programmer
digital recording
[see 290, 291]

169

television
TV set
screen size
remote control
teletext
rental
cable
video recorder
video cassette
[see 290, 291]

170

tobacconist
tobacco
pouch
packet
pipes
cigarettes
cigars
matches
lighters
fuel
flints
pipe-cleaners

171

department store
floors
basement
lift
escalator
assistant
cash-point
receipt
paper bag
carrier

172

card shop
greeting
birthday
engagement
anniversary
wedding
new baby
congratulations
Christmas
get well
retirement
condolence

173

hairdresser
ladies
gentlemen
hairstyle
shampoo
haircream
waves
perm
drier
curls
trim
haircut
[see 69, 119]

174

clothing (men's)
tailor
suits
trousers
jackets
overcoats
jumpers
socks
vest
pants
ties
hats
gloves
[see 58-66, 121]

175

clothing (women's)
dress
blouse
skirt
trousers
jumper
sweater
lingerie
underwear
tights
stockings
[see 58-66, 121]

176

wine store
off-licence
red wine
white wine
sparkling
champagne
rosé
sherry
port
whisky
gin
brandy
beer
lager
bottle
can
case

shopping

177
shops
manager
supervisor
assistant
cashier
buyer
helpful
polite
obliging
serve
queue
entrance
exit
opening hours
window display
counter
shelves
scales
weigh
[see 84]

178
market
open
stalls
covered
shops
pedestrian precinct
arcade
galleria
[see 84]

179
delivery
order
deposit
deliver
supply
stock
carton
crate
parcel
van
[see 84]

180
purchasing
purchase
shopping list
purse
wallet
pocket
money
bank notes
silver
copper
coins
pound
pence
cash
hire-purchase
H.P.
cheque
banker's card
credit card
till
pay
paid
V.A.T.
change
receipt
[see 84]

181
price
dear
expensive
cheap
inexpensive
bargain
offer
sale
reduced
discount
bill
buy
bought
purchase
coupon
stamps
receipt
credit note
refund
[see 84]

182
carrying
carry
carrier

carried
bag
basket
trolley
case
parcel
packet
package
paper
gift wrap
stick
tape
[see 84]

recreation

183
play
game
chase
dodge
catch
caught
race
run
running
follow-my-leader
hide and seek
dance
skip
rope
swing
jump
leapfrog

184
park
swings
roundabouts
slides
climbing frame
boating lake
ball
bat
field
pitch
net
court
racket
team
side
innings
turn
[see 225]

185
indoors
bricks
blocks
jigsaw
cards
dominoes
chess
draughts
ludo
Monopoly
puzzles
snap
soldiers
doll's house
marbles
darts
dartboard
skittles

contd.

table-tennis
quoits
[see 160]

186

outdoors
bicycle
tricycle
scooter
pram
roller skates
ice-skates
skateboard
kite
fly
tent
climbing frame
paddling pool
[see 160, 184]

187

television
set
switch
remote control
picture
programme
Radio Times
TV Times
channel
cartoon
puppets
quizzes
western
detective
mystery
serial
musical
variety show
magician
conjurer
pop group
science fiction
[see 169, 290]

188

hi-fi
video recorder
videotape
record-player
tape recorder
compact disc player
C.D.
L.P.
single
cassette
tuner
speaker
[see 168, 291]

189

theatre
stage
backstage
wings
curtain
lights
scenery
actors
play
comedy
tragedy
audience

clap
applause
programme
interval
pantomime
fairy godmother
principal boy
dame
villain
happy ending
exit

190

concert
hall
orchestra
band
choir
soloist
pianist
players
instruments
conductor
baton
symphony
concerto
chorus
organ
opera
ballet
mime
encore
ovation

191

cinema
box office
big screen
usherette
film
movie
stars
exciting
cartoon
special effects
soundtrack

192

circus
caravan
parade
big top
ring-master
acts
clowns
acrobats
horses
bareback riders
jugglers
trapeze artists
somersault
twist
catch
safety-net
tightrope
balance
animals
perform
hoops
cages
menagerie

193

fair
carnival
tents
roundabouts
rides
rifle shoot
prize
coconut-shies
helter-skelter
dodgems
stall
fortune-teller
bingo

194

books
picture
story
poetry
fairy tale
adventure
mystery
detective
animal
western
sport
science fiction
novel
play
paperback

contd.

fiction
non-fiction
information
school book
textbook
dictionary
encyclopaedia
volume
reference
historical
biography
autobiography
anthology
title
jacket
cover
page
chapter
contents
illustrations
notes
index
library
[see 105, 106]

sport

195

general
amateur
professional
league
city
county
national
international
championship
Olympics
record
winner
medal
match
team
players
opponents
referee
umpire
whistle
pitch
goal
crowd
spectators
supporters
score

196

football
soccer
association
strip
shirt
number
shorts
goalkeeper
defend
forward
striker
captain
linesman
flag
centre
corner
penalty
goal post
header
dribble
tackle
foul
free kick
nil
half-time
full-time
trainer
manager
substitute
home
away

197

rugby football
union
league
fifteen
thirteen
scrum
line-out
touch
try
dummy
tackle
penalty
points

198

cricket
ground
pitch
wicket
stumps
bails
new ball
bowler
over
run-up
spin
batsman
crease
runs
boundary
bye
fielder
wicket-keeper
gloves
pads
out
not out
catch
caught
stumped
run out
century
innings
declared

199

hockey
hockey stick
centre
bully-off
corner
shooter
wing
foul

200

athletics
stadium
meeting
events
track
field
heats
starting gun
blocks
sprint
lanes
bend
bell
lap
back straight
finishing-line
timing
stop-watch
record
personal best
marathon
high-jump
long-jump
pit
sand
take-off
shot-put
hammer
discus
javelin
pole-vault
hurdles
steeplechase

201
netball
net
goal
shooter
pass
foul
court
centre

202
rounders
bat
post
base
rounder
bowler
backstop
pitch

203
swimming
pool
lanes
costume
badge
cap
dive
free-style
crawl
breast stroke
butterfly stroke
back stroke

204
tennis
court
net
racket
racquet
service
let
fault
umpire
line judge
forehand
backhand
return
volley
lob
smash
slice
singles
doubles
game
set
match

205
table-tennis
bat
serve
fault
return
topspin
backspin
backflip
lob
chop
smash

206
show-jumping
jumps
poles

faults
time faults
clear round
double fence
triple fence
wall
water jump
jump-off

207

motor-racing
pits
driver
starting grid
accelerate
gears
bend
corner
chicane
straight
lap
braking
breakdown
pit-stop
wheel-change
chequered flag

208

cycle racing
headgear
jersey
number
hill-climb
gears
freewheel
sponge
endurance
milk race
pursuit
sprint

209

fishing
bank
stool
rod
line
bait
hook
net
bite
strike
reel
weight
waders
fly-fishing
cast
coarse fishing
[see 116, 267]

210

golf
course
clubs
wood
iron
tee
drive
shot
fairway
bunker
green
flag
hole
putt
par
bogie
birdie
eagle

211

boxing
ring
ropes
referee
seconds
boxers
gloves
timekeeper
rounds
bell
foul
knockdown
count
points
knockout

212

wrestling
wrestlers
ropes
holds
fall

contd.

submission
knockout
catchweights
team tag
referee

213

snooker
umpire
table
baize
pockets
balls
baulk
white
reds
colours
cue
miscue
chalk
tip
break
pot
points
foul stroke
plant
frame

environment

214

universe
stars
galaxy
constellation
sun
solar system
planet
moon
axis
rotate
orbit
meteor
meteorite
comet
pulsar
quasar
nova
black hole
astronomer
observatory
telescope
reflector

215

planet Earth
ocean
continent
sea
island
archipelago
atoll
peninsula
isthmus
bight
strait
gulf
mountain
range
pass
valley
volcano
erupt
molten rock
lava
canyon
gorge
fiord
ravine
plain
grassland
prairie
steppe
pampas
forest
jungle
swamp
tundra
permafrost
icefield
icecap
glacier
iceberg
desert
sand
dune
oasis
mirage
[see 26]

216

rock
sandstone
limestone
granite
slate

chalk
shale
flint
[see 224]

217

minerals
iron
copper
tin
lead
zinc
aluminium
nickel
platinum
gold
silver
diamond
emerald
ruby
sapphire

218

country
fields
lanes
hedges
ditches
crops
trees
woods
flowers
meadows
plain

heath
moor
common
lake
pond
marsh
stream
river
hill
mountain
valley
animals
birds
insects
farms
hamlets
villages
[see127]

219

town
city
street
road
crossing
pavement
bus
station
railway
traffic
warden
parking
car park
garage
yellow lines
policeman

contd.

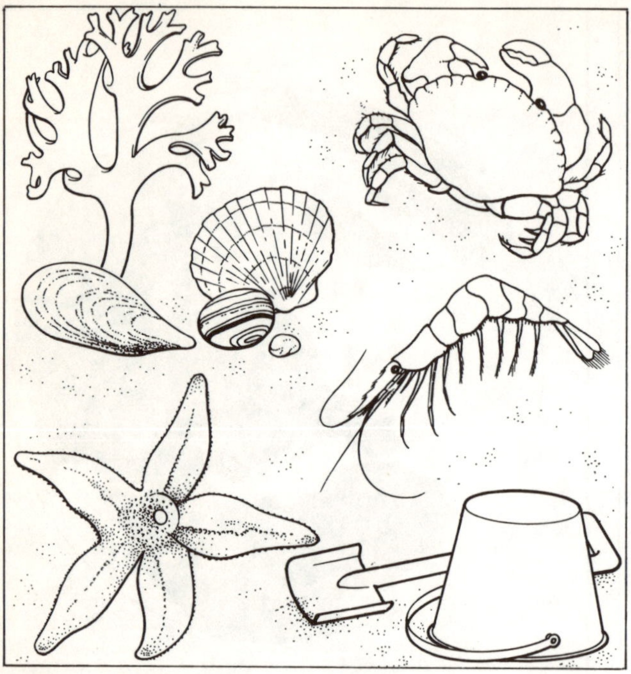

department store
shop
shopping precinct
buildings
skyscraper
café
snack bar
restaurant
hotel
cinema
theatre
concert hall
town hall
church
cathedral
museum
library
bank
office
police station
fire station
hospital
ambulance depot
market
park
gardens
[see 226]

220

seaside
shore
waves
surf
breakers
paddle
splash
bathe
shallow
deep
swim
float
tide
current
salt
rock pool
net
catch
crab
shrimp
cockles
mussels
starfish
seaweed
beach
pebbles
shells
sandcastle
bucket
spade
picnic
deckchair
rug
sunburnt
donkey
Punch and Judy
canoe
yacht
sail
crew
pier
promenade
harbour
quay
fishing boats
[see 243-248]

221

underwater
skin-diver
wetsuit
flippers
mask
aqualung
snorkel
oxygen bottle
pressure-gauge
wristwatch
compass
torch
depth
bottom
explore
rocks
reef
seaweed
wreck
sand
mud
fish
shoal
dive
swim
surface
[see 248]

222

farm
dairy
arable
stock
poultry
farmhouse
farmyard
barn
hay
straw
cowshed
milk-cooler
eggs
haystack
pigsty
trough
orchard
paddock
tractor
plough
furrow
seed
plant
manure
fertiliser
spray
crops
grain silo
silage
corn
vegetables
harvest
combine
fence
hedge
gate
animals
cattle
sheep
graze
[see 127, 128, 262]

223

mountain
range
peak
summit
cairn
rocks
cliff
scree
ridge
pass
slope
gradient
height
sheep
cloud
mist
breeze
wind
view
panorama
spring
rivulet
waterfall
[see 216]

224

river
source
spring
stream
brook
shallow
deep
flow

contd.

rapids
cataract
rocks
waterfall
meander
bank
erosion
bed
boulder
silt
weeds
rushes
salmon ladder
voles
water rats
otters
bridge
boat
ford
ferry
stepping-stones
tributary
confluence
oxbow-lake
backwater
torrent
in spate
flood
weir
mouth
estuary
[see 218, 223]

225

park
grass
shrubs
trees
shade
flowers
path
lake
swans
geese
ducks
playground
swings
bandstand
gates
[see 184, 219]

226

buildings
abbey
monastery
convent
art gallery
museum
library
swimming pool
bank
building society
cathedral
church
chapel
temple
synagogue
castle
monument
school
college
university
theatre
concert hall
cinema
department store
factory
hospital
football ground
hotel
market
office
skyscraper
palace
post office
railway station
bus station
stadium
telephone exchange
town hall
civic centre
[see 90-93, 219]

transport

227

road
street
avenue
drive
lane
by-pass
main road
trunk road
bus lane
cycle path
diversion
[see 86]

228

motorway
hard shoulder
junction
entrance
exit
service area
underpass
overpass
contra-flow
repairs
cones

229

features
T-junction
fork
crossroads
level crossing
pedestrian-crossing
zebra-crossing
pelican-crossing
roundabout
dual carriageway
traffic lights
traffic jam
tailback
layby

230

repairs
tarmac
digger
bulldozer
excavator
spreader
dumper
roadroller
roadworks
[see 129]

231

vehicle
car
saloon
taxi
limousine
sports car
racing car
estate car
hatchback
lorry
bus
coach
caravan
[see 115]

232

parts
wheels
tyres
tread
air pressure
dashboard
speedometer
radio
cassette player
stereo
windscreen
wipers
steering wheel
seat belts
boot
bonnet
radiator
headlights
dipped
main beam
fog lamps

contd.

rear lights
reversing lights
number plate
licence disc
A.A.
R.A.C.
[see 115]

233

garage
filling station
petrol
gallon
litre
oil
dipstick
water
battery
charge
car wash

petrol pumps
self-service
attendant
tank
spare parts
[see 98]

234

bus
single-decker
double-decker
pay-as-you-enter
bus stop
fare stage
number
destination
terminus
conductor
fare
ticket

bus station
[see 86]

235

truck
van
lorry
tailboard
cab
tachograph
artic
articulated truck
container lorry
trailer
juggernaut
roadtanker
C.B. radio
fire-engine
ambulance
dust-cart
police car
siren
[see 87]

236

motorbike
crash helmet
motorcyclist
pedals
gears
mudguards
handlebars
steer
saddle

237

animal transport
horse
pony
reins
stirrup
trot
canter
gallop
pony trek
stables
groom
harness
tackle
fodder
ox
camel
llama
donkey
mule
elephant

238

pedestrian
walk
hike
boots
anorak
rucksack
route
footpath
compass
[see 60]

239

rail
railway station
stationmaster
platform
booking office
fare
ticket
ticket-collector
inspector
baggage
luggage
freight
porter
taxi-rank
left luggage
[see 88]

240

railway journey
track
rails
sleepers
points
signals
signal box
electric
wires
bridge
viaduct
tunnel
level crossing
siding
engine sheds
turntable

241

locomotive
engine
diesel
steam
electric
pantograph
rail bus
coupling
buffers
shunting
[see 88]

242

rolling stock
carriage
coach
car
compartment
non-smoking
corridor
buffet-car
dining-car
sleeping-car
wagon
truck
brake van
guard's van
local train
commuter train
inter-city
stopping train
express

243
water transport
liner
cruise
oil tanker
cargo liner
coaster
car ferry
rowing boat
raft
lifeboat
motor boat
speedboat
powerboat
yacht
hovercraft
launch
lightship
canoe
dinghy
[see 111, 112]

244
ship
deck
bridge
cabin
porthole
bow
stern
winch
hold
cargo
funnel
smoke-stack
radio shack
anchor
propeller
screw
rudder
steer
derrick
davit
navigate
horizon
pilot
port
starboard

245
yacht
sail
rope
mast
pulley
tiller
boom
hawser
tie-up
flag
spinnaker
lifejacket

246
crew
captain
skipper
pilot
bosun
engineer
officer
seaman
coxswain
navigator
[see 116, 117]

247
port
harbour
quay
bollard
shipyard
crane
dock
dry dock
graving dock
floating dock
pier
jetty
landing-stage
alongside
loading
unloading
fork-lift truck
customs
duty
passport
[see 111, 112, 116, 117]

248
sea
ocean
tide
waves
breakers

sandbanks
rocks
channel
lighthouse
buoy
calm
rough
seasick
capsize
drown
lifebelt
[see 111, 112]

249

canal
bank
lock
lock-keeper
gate
barge
bargee
narrowboat
towpath
tunnel
swing bridge
motor-launch
houseboat
punt
canoe
paddles

250

airline
aeroplane
aircraft

airliner
helicopter
rotor
jet engine
flight
fly
flew
wings
air-brakes
fuselage
undercarriage
landing wheels
tail
fin
nose
view
fields
towns
coastline
clouds
captain
co-pilot
navigator

air hostess
steward
stewardess
galley
reclining seats
seat-belt
turbulence
lifejacket
inflate
cabin pressure
oxygen
emergency door
emergency chute

251

airport
control tower
air traffic controller
radar
terminal
customs
declare

contd.

passport
security check
runway
flight path
hangar

252

route
great circle
compass
distance
direction
navigate
airspeed
knots
miles
kilometres
E.T.A.
estimated time
of arrival

253

altitude
height
climb
ascend
ascent
descend
descent
approach
radio
radar
auto-pilot

254

balloon
hot air
burn
gas
inflate
basket
ascent
wind
altitude
drift
descent
landing

255

space transport
rocket
capsule
shuttle
launching pad
launch
countdown
lift-off
blast-off
module
orbit
mission control

256

astronaut
cosmonaut
spacesuit
weightlessness
zero gravity
space walk
life-cord
space laboratory
space docking
satellite-launching
solar panels

257

lunar expedition
moon-track
moon-orbit
dark side
moon-landing
retro-rockets
moon-rock
moon-dust
zero atmosphere
moon-mobile
less gravity
booster-rockets
earth track
re-entry
heat shield
parachutes
touch-down
splash-down
recovery
shuttle-landing

nature

258

weather
atmosphere
stratosphere
ozone layer
clouds
cirrus
cumulus
nimbus
breeze
wind
gust
gale
whirlwind
tornado
monsoon
cyclone
anti-cyclone
typhoon
hurricane
Beaufort Scale
rain
rainbow
drizzle
shower
downpour
cloudburst
sleet
snow
blizzard
storm
thunder
lightning
frost
frozen
ice
black ice
icicle
fog
freezing fog
mist
smog

259

meteorology
meteorological office
barometer
barograph
air pressure
high
low
isobars
thermometer
temperature
humidity
visibility
wind gauge
rain gauge
weather vane
forecast
depression
cold front
warm front
hard frost
freezing
temperate
mild
clear
changeable
unsettled
stormy
damp
cloudy
dull
overcast
humid
fine
sunny
dry
drought
heatwave

260

temperature
hot
sweltering
blazing
searing
burning
baking
parched
steaming
boiling
blistering
torrid
scorching
sweating
tropical
oppressive
sultry
humid
clammy
close
warm
temperate
cool
chilly
keen
sharp
cold
bleak
bitter
raw
frigid
freezing
frosty
crisp
icy
frozen
glacial
arctic

261

pets
vet
veterinary
surgeon
dog
puppy
cat
kitten
rabbit
hamster
guinea pig
gerbil
white mouse
budgerigar
parrot
pony
horse
foal
donkey
tortoise
[see 83]

262

domestic animals
sheep
ewe
ram
lamb
bull
cow
heifer
calf
calves
goat
kid
pig
hog
sow
piglet
hen
cock
[see 83]

263

wild creatures (Britain)
rabbit
hare
squirrel
hedgehog
mole
fox
bat
deer
stag
badger
ferret
rat
weasel
otter
seal
adder
grass snake

264

wild creatures (overseas)
lion
tiger
leopard
cheetah
jaguar
bear
grizzly bear
polar bear
panda
koala bear
wolf
dingo
hyena
jackal
beaver
elephant
giraffe
camel
hippopotamus
rhinoceros
buffalo
bison
zebra
wildebeest
kangaroo
wallaby
reindeer
caribou
moose
antelope
gazelle
llama
gorilla
chimpanzee
orang-utan
baboon
gibbon
monkey
bush baby

265

birds (Britain)
sparrow
starling
robin
thrush
blackbird
tit
crow
rook
magpie
jackdaw
pigeon
swallow
swift
martin
wagtail
owl
cuckoo
woodpecker
finch
jay
wren
lark
duck
swan
goose
moorhen
coot
kingfisher
heron
gull
cormorant
puffin
hawk
kestrel
falcon

contd.

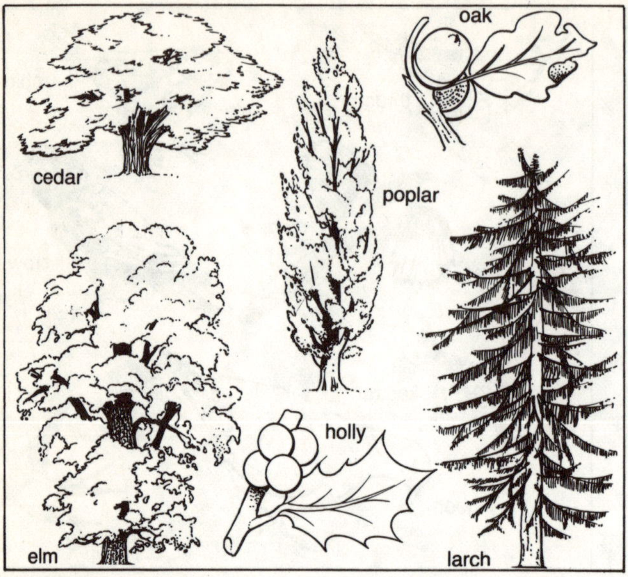

eagle
pheasant
grouse
partridge
quail
peacock

266

birds (overseas)
budgerigar
canary
cockatoo
macaw
parrot
mynah
parakeet
ostrich
emu
stork
crane
flamingo
cassowary
kiwi
kookaburra
lyre bird
bird of paradise
humming bird
toucan
pelican
penguin
hornbill
vulture
condor
albatross

267

water creatures
stickleback
minnow
trout
salmon
eel
pike
roach
carp
tench
bass
bream
perch
dace
gudgeon
cod
herring
plaice
sole
haddock
halibut
mackerel
whiting
pilchard
sardine
sprat
tuna
catfish
dogfish
flounder
skate
octopus
squid
flying fish
swordfish
shark
dolphin
porpoise
whale
turtle
terrapin
crab
lobster

shrimp
oyster
cockle
mussel
amphibian
frog
toad
newt
tadpole
salamander
[see 116, 149]

268

invertebrates
fly
blowfly
bluebottle
wasp
bee
hornet
cranefly
daddy-longlegs
butterfly
moth
caterpillar
grub
maggot
earthworm
ant
beetle
cockroach
centipede
dragonfly
ladybird
gnat
earwig
flea
louse
lice
mosquito
grasshopper
cricket
greenfly
blackfly
spider
tarantula
black widow
silkworm
praying mantis
stick insect

269

reptiles
smooth snake
grass snake
adder
viper
lizard
tortoise
slow-worm
crocodile
alligator
chameleon
iguana
python
cobra
rattlesnake
puff adder
mamba
boa constrictor
anaconda

270

trees
oak
horse chestnut
sweet chestnut
sycamore
fir
pine
elm
beech
ash
plane
lime
birch
poplar
hawthorn
willow
yew
holly
laburnum
apple
pear
plum
cherry
hazel
walnut
conifer
evergreen
deciduous
[see 184, 218, 225]

271

gardens
hedge
lawn

contd.

daisy
dandelion
border
rockery
flower-bed
path
plants
seeds
seedling
annual
perennial
fruit
orchard
flowers
cuttings
foliage
weeds
compost
manure
fertiliser
leaves
vegetables
rubbish
burn
bonfire
[see 15, 138]

272

air
oxygen
nitrogen
breathe
lungs
atmosphere
stratosphere
air pressure
barometer
bird
soar
glide
air current
ventilation
fan
draught
air-conditioning
air pump
pneumatic tyre
inflate
football
balloon
air-bed
air-brakes
aircraft
airship
aeroplane
aerosol
helicopter
autogiro
glider
kite
parachute
hovercraft
aqualung
snorkel
airtight
vacuum
suction
exhaust
windmill
wind pump
diving-bell
airlock
diver
air-line

273

water
hydrogen
oxygen
ocean
sea
tide
wave
river
stream
brook
weir
waterfall
canal
lock
pond
pool
lake

274

rain
drizzle
shower
downpour
cloudburst
flood
deluge
hail
sleet
snow
blizzard
ice
icicle
cloud
[see 258, 259]

275

mist
fog
vapour
dew
steam
sweat
condensation
evaporate
dank
humid
humidity

276

wet
soaked
saturated
drenched
dripping
wringing
moist
damp

277

waterworks
reservoir
dam
well
artesian
water-level
filter
purity
softening
pumping-station

fountain
jets
pipe
main
aqueduct
channel
culvert
drain
sewer
hydrant

278

domestic water
tap
tank
cistern
overflow
burst
stopcock
radiator
water-softener
hard water
soft water
water-bottle
quench
water-bed
watering-can
hose
jet
spray
[see 10, 13, 14]

279

fire
kindle
smoke
spark
smoulder
glow
flicker
burn
crackle
blaze

contd.

blazing
camp-fire
bonfire
forest fire
beacon
flame
flammable
non-flammable
fumes
singe
melt
scorch
char
charred
ashes
cinders
flint
friction
lighter

match
ignite
ignition
combustion
conflagration
incinerate
cremate
cremation
fire-brigade
fire-station
fireman
axe
fire-engine
fire-hydrant
fire-alarm
fire-extinguisher
siren
[see 77]

time

280

measurement
century
decade
year
leap year
month
fortnight
week
weekend
day
hour
minute
second
millisecond

281

season
spring
summer
autumn
winter
Christmas
New Year
Easter
Whitsun
midsummer
Halloween
equinox
solstice
bonfire night
term
half-term
holiday
annual

282

calendar
January (31 days)
February (28 or 29)
March (31)
April (30)
May (31)
June (30)
July (31)
August (31)
September (30)
October (31)
November (30)
December (31)

283

days
Sunday
Monday
Tuesday
Wednesday
Thursday
Friday
Saturday
today
yesterday
tomorrow
tonight
this morning
this afternoon
this evening
last week
this week
next week

284

daytime
daily
daybreak
dawn
sunrise
morning
noon
midday
afternoon
evening
sunset
dusk
twilight
night
midnight

285

the clock
o'clock
quarter past
half past
quarter to
chimes
Big Ben
BBC pips
fast
slow
timetable
24-hour clock
period
session
moment

286

when?
before
after
early
late
now
then
first
last
past
present
future
modern
old-fashioned
out-of-date
ancient
antique
obsolete

287

how often?
always
ever
frequently
regularly
sometimes
infrequently
occasionally
seldom
never

288
how soon?
instantly
immediately
promptly
punctually
quickly
swiftly
rapidly
speedily
suddenly
afterwards
later
some time
by and by

communications

289
language
speech
speak
talk
say
tell
relate
mention
inform
announce
describe
explain
advise
suggest
warn
order
exclaim
call
shout
yell
whisper
greet
discuss
discussion
argue
argument
converse
conversation
debate
chat
chatter
gossip
ask
request
demand
enquire
question
listen
hear

290
television
mast
studio
broadcast
producer
sound-recorder
director
floor-manager
announcer
dubbing-mixer
camera
rostrum camera
newsreader
picture
channel
colour
contrast
sound
video
aerial
station
programme
news
comedy
play
documentary
serial
musical
ballet
opera
[see 169, 187]

291
radio
transistor
receiver
portable
battery
tuner
music centre
tuning
wavelength
long wave
medium wave
short wave
frequency

F.M.
A.M.
V.H.F.
aerial
stereo
speakers
[see 168, 188]

292

telephone
mouthpiece
earpiece
call
bell
ring
answer
exchange
code
number
dial
dialling
S.T.D.
tone
engaged
cut off
disconnected
long-distance
overseas
reverse-charge call
international
cable phone
radio phone
cordless phone
satellite phone
directory
yellow pages

kiosk
coin-box
pay-phone
credit-card phone
insert
pips
emergency
999

293

letters
paper
writing
typing
envelope
address
post code
stamp
first class
second class
airmail
surface mail
franking
postmark
collection
delivery
postbox
pillar-box
by return
recorded delivery
registered post
mail van
[see 73, 161]

294

newspaper
headline
news
report
photograph
article
review

contd.

advertisement
letter
editorial
sport
cartoon
weather
crossword
stop-press
column
edition
daily
weekly
Sunday
national
provincial
local
editor
edit
reporter
journalist
contributor
photographer

delivery van
newsagent
paper-round
magazine
comic
journal
[see 105, 106]

law

295

law-making
parliament
House of Commons
House of Lords
debate
speaker
bill
act
government
cabinet
opposition
backbencher
royal assent

296

police
policeman
policewoman
C.I.D.
detective
constable
sergeant
inspector
superintendent
chief constable
police station
interview-room
caution
arrest
charge
statement
release
bail
cell
custody
[see 76]

297

court
bench
dock
witness-box
summons

case
accused
prisoner
trial
prosecute
prosecution
defend
defence
judge
magistrate
clerk of court
jury
verdict
innocent
remand
acquitted
discharged
guilty
sentence
[see 107, 108]

298

punishment
probation
fine
imprisonment
gaol
jail

299

crime
criminal
fraud
theft
thief
thieves
burglar
burglary
assault
injury
manslaughter
homicide
murder

basic descriptions

300

size (small)
infinitesimal
microscopic
minute
diminutive
tiny
miniature
minuscule
puny
trifling
pygmy
midget
dwarf
bonsai
undersized
stunted
shrunken
dainty
petite
minor

301

size (large)
great
huge
voluminous
elephantine
vast
lofty
tremendous
giant
massive
mighty
enormous
extensive
colossal
prodigious
gigantic
gargantuan
immense
towering
mammoth
monstrous
boundless
immeasurable
infinite

302

shape (regular)
level
straight
flat
round
curved
arched
circular

contd.

semi-circular
oval
elliptical
sphere
spherical
conical
pyramid
cylinder
cylindrical
symmetrical
balanced
square
rectangle
rectangular
triangle
triangular
hexagonal
octagonal
spiral
wavy
shapely
proportionate
upright
vertical
horizontal
diagonal
concave
convex
plane

303

shape (irregular)
bent
askew
crooked
twisted
rugged
mis-shapen
distorted
mutilated
disfigured
deformed
shapeless

304

colour
tint
hue
cast
shade
tinge
tone
bloom
pigment
dye
paint

305

dark
black
ebony
pitch
soot
jet
coal
sombre

306

light
snow
chalk
ivory
pearl
silver
cream
bleached

307

red
scarlet
crimson
vermilion
magenta
blush
blood
rose
pink
ruddy
rouge
russet
ruby
maroon

308

blue
cobalt
indigo
azure
sky
navy
ultramarine
turquoise
sapphire

309

green
jade
emerald
leaf
apple
grass
olive
sage
bottle

310

yellow
gold
lemon
topaz
primrose
buff
saffron
orange

311

brown
bronze
chestnut
tan
rust
fawn
auburn
beige

312

purple
violet
mauve
lilac

313

textures
smooth
rough
coarse
fine
fluffy
hairy
furry
prickly
sharp
blunt
jagged
spiky
serrated
indented
porous
cellular
[see 48]

INDEX

*The numbers refer to the section numbers, not to the page numbers. The words and numbers which are in **bold** type are the section headings. The words and numbers which are in ordinary type are the words in the lists.*

A.A. 232
abbey 226
ablaze 43
accelerate 207
accident 34
accountant 124
accounts 124
accused 108, 297
acid 49
acquitted 297
acrid 47
acrobat 192
act 192, 295
actor 189
add 22
adder 263, 269
address 293
adult 17
adventure 194
adventurous 54
advertisement 294
advise 289
aerial 290, 291
aeroplane 250
aerosol 272
affectionate 70
afraid 53
after 286
afternoon 284
afterwards 288
ailing 32
air 272
air-bed 272
air-brakes 250, 272
air-conditioning 272
aircraft 250, 272
air current 272
air hostess 250
airing cupboard 13
air-line 272
airline 250
airliner 250
airlock 272
air mail 161, 293
airman 110
airport 251
air pressure 232, 259, 272
air pump 272
airship 272
air speed 252
air-tight 272
air traffic controller 251
albatross 266
album 168
alight 43
alligator 269
alongside 247
altitude 253, 254
aluminium 217
always 287
A.M. 291
amateur 195
amble 41
ambulance 34, **78**, 235
ambulance depot 219
amphibian 269
amplifier 31, 168
anaconda 269
anaesthetic 34
ancestor 1
anchor 244
ancient 24, 286
anger 52
angry 52
animals 83, 192, 194, 218, 222, 262
animal transport 237
ankle 37
anniversary 172
announce 289
announcer 290
annoyed 52
annual 271, 281
anorak 58, 238
answer 21, 292
ant 268
antelope 264
anthology 194
anthracite 74
antibiotic 33
anticyclone 258

antique 286
antiseptic 33
anxious 53
apartment 7
apparatus 23
appeal 108
appearance 71
appetising 49
applause 189
apple 146, 270, 309
appliance 77
apprentice 130
apprenticeship 130
approach 253
apricot 146
April 282
aqualung 221, 272
aqueduct 277
arable 127, 222
arcade 178
arched 302
archipelago 215
architect 91
architecture 91
arctic 260
argue 289
argument 289
arithmetic 22
arm 37
armchair 9
armour 24
aroma 47
aroused 55
arrest 296
arrogant 70
art 27
artery 38
artesian 277
art gallery 226
artic 235
article 105, 294
articulated truck 235
ascend 253
ascent 253, 254
ash 270, 279
ask 289
askew 303
assault 299
assembling 115
assembly 101
assembly-line 115
assistant 84, 171, 177
association (football) 196
asthma 33
astride 30
astronaut 256
astronomer 214
ate 144
athletics 200
atlas 26
atmosphere 258, 272
atoll 215
atomic energy 135
attack 110
attendant 233
attentive 56
attic 14
attracted 56
aubergine 145
auburn 69, 311
audience 189
August 282
aunt 2
author 126
autobiography 194
autogiro 272
auto-pilot 253
autumn 281
avenue 227
avocado 146
away 196
axe 77, 279
axis 214
azure 308

baboon 264
baby 3
baby food 162
baby-gro 65
baby wear 65
bachelor 4
backbencher 295
backbone 39
back flip 205
background 120
backhand 204
backspin 205
backstage 189
backstop 202
back straight 200
backstroke 203
backwater 224
bacon 148, 158
badge 203
badger 263
bag 159, 182
baggage 239, 251

bail 296
bails 198
bait 209
baize 213
baked 152
baker 156
baking 260
balance 124, 192
balanced 302
bald 69
ball 184, 213
ballet 190, 290
balloon 254, 272
balsa wood 28
banana 146
band 31, 190
bandage 34, 82, 162
bandstand 225
bang 45
banisters 9
bank 209, 219, 224, 226, 249
banker's card 180
bank note 180
bar 159
bareback rider 192
bargain 181
barge 249
bargee 249
barley 147
barn 222
barograph 259
barometer 259, 272
barrister 108
base 202
basement 171
basin 141
basket 182, 254
bass 267
bat 184, 202, 205, 263
bath 13, 114
bathe 220
bathmat 13
bathroom 13
baton 190
batsman 198
batteries 167
battery 23, 233, 291
battle 24
baulk 213
B.B.C. pips 285
beach 220
beacon 279
beam 89
bean 145
bear 264
beard 69
beat 38, 76
Beaufort Scale 258
beaver 264
bed 164, 224
bedroom 12
bedspread 12
bee 268
beech 270
beef 148, 158
beefburger 148
beer 176
beetle 268
beetroot 145
before 286
beige 311
bell 19, 86, 200, 211, 292
belt 59
bench 109, **135**, 297
bend 28, 200, 207
bent 67,303
beret 62
best friend 6
best man 4
beverages 151, 157
bicycle 186
bidet 13
Big Ben 285
bight 215
big screen 191
big top 192
bikini 59
bill 123, 154, 181, 295
bin 75, 165
bin bag 75
binder 142
bingo 193
biography 194
birch 270
bird 218, 272
birdie 210
bird of paradise 266
birds (Britain) 265
birds (overseas) 266
biro 18
birth 3
birthday 3, 172
biscuit 153
bison 264
bite 209
bitter 49, 260

black 69, 305
blackberry 146
blackbird 265
blackboard 18, 100
black fly 268
black hole 214
black ice 258
black widow 268
bland 49
blanket 12
blast furnace 113
blast-off 255
blaze 279
blazer 58
blazing 260, 279
bleached 306
bleak 260
blender 11, 141
blind 8
blinding 43
blistering 260
blizzard 258, 274
blocks 159, 185, 200
blond(e) 69
blood 38, 307
blood-test 35
bloom 304
blouse 59, 175
blow-drier 119
blow fly 268
blow-lamp 94, 95
blow-torch 98
blue 308
blue bottle 268
blunt 313
blurred 44
blush 307
boa constrictor 269
board 89
boastful 70
boat 116, 224
boating lake 184
body 37
bogie 210
boil 102
boiled 152
boiler 10, 94
boiler-house 16
boiler-room 103
boiling 260
bold 54
bollard 247
bolster 12
bolt 98, 115, 136
bones 39
bonfire 271, 279
bonfire night 281
bonnet 65, 232
bonsai 300
book 18, 100, 105, **194**
bookcase 9, 18
booking office 239
boom 45, 245
booster-rocket 257
boot 232
bootees 65
boots 60, 238
border 271
bored 57
boredom 57
born 3
borrowing 126
bosun 245
bottle 72, 82, 155, 157, 176, 309
bottle-opener 141
bottom 221
bought 181
boulder 224
boundary 198
boundless 301
bouquet 166
bow 244
bowler 198, 202
bow-tie 63
box 159
boxer 211
boxing 211
box office 191
bra 61
brace and bit 136
braces 59
brake-van 242
braking 207
bran 147
brandy 176
brave 54
brawny 67
bread 11, 150, 156
break 19, 213
breakdown 207, 332
breakers 220, 248
breakfast 144
bream 267
breast-bone 39
breast stroke 203
breathe 272
breeze 223, 258
brick 7
bricklayer 93

bricks 160, 185
bride 4
bridegroom 4
bridesmaid 4
bridge 224, 240, 244
brief 107
briefs 61
bright 43
brilliant 43
Britain 263, 265
brittle 48
broadcast 290
broccoli 145
broken 34
bronchitis 33
bronze 311
bronzed 68
brooch 64
brook 224, 273
broom 137, 138
brother 1
brother-in-law 2
brown 69, **311**
brush 13, 27, 95, 104, 137
bubble bath 13
bucket 137, 220
buckle 59
budgerigar 261, 266
budget 124
buff 310
buffalo 264
buffers 241
buffet-car 242
build **67**, 208
building 16, **92**, 219, **226**
building site 92
building society 226
bulb 167
bull 262
bulldozer 230
bully-off 199
bun 153, 156
bunch 166
bungalow 7
bunk 12, 164
bunker 210
buoy 248
burglar 299
burglary 299
buried 5
burn 254, 271, 279
burner 10, 23
burning 260
burst 94, 278
bus **86**, 219, 231, **234**
bush baby 264
bus lane 227
bus station 226, 234
bus stop 234
butcher **158**
butter 150, 155
butterfly 268
butterfly stroke 203
button 64
buttonhole 64
buy 181
buyer 177
by and by 288
bye 198
by-pass 227
by return 293
byte 140
cab 235
cabbage 145
cabin 244
cabinet 9, 295
cabin pressure 250
cable 131, 167, 169
cable phone 292
café 87, **154**, 219
cafeteria 154
cage 114, 192
cagoule 58
cairn 223
cake 153, 156
calculate 22
calculator 22, 124, 139
calendar **282**
calf 262
call 289, 292
calm 248
calories 143
calves 262
camel 237, 264
camera 120, 290
campfire 279
can 176
canal 26, **249**, 273
canary 266
canoe 220, 243, 249
can-opener 141
canter 237
canyon 215
cap 62, 203
caper 42
capital 26
capital letter 21
capsize 248

capsule 255
captain 196, 246, 250
captivated 56
car 160, 231, 242
caravan 7, 192, 231
car-bodies 115
carbohydrate 143
cardboard 28
cardigan 59
cards 185
card shop 172
caretaker 17, **103**
car ferry 111, 243
cargo 111, 117, 244
cargo liner 243
caribou 264
carnival 193
carp 267
car park 219
carpenter 89
carpet 8, 164
carriage 242
carried 182
carrier 171, 182
carrots 145
carry 182
carrying 182
carton 72, 155, 179
cartoon 187, 191, 294
cartwheel 30
car wash 233
car worker 115
case 107, 176, 182, 297
cash 180
cashier 124, 177
cash-point 171
cassette 140, 188
cassette deck 168
cassette player 232
cassette recorder 20
cassowary 266
cast 209, 304
casting 113
castle 24, 226
cast off 29
cast on 29
cat 261
catalogue 126
cataract 224
catch 30, 116, 183, 192, 198, 220
catchweights 212
caterpillar 268
catfish 267
cathedral 219, 226
cattle 222
caught 183, 198
cauliflower 145
caution 296
C.B. radio 235
C.D. 188
celery 145
cell 296
cellular 313
cemetery 5
centimetre 22
centipede 268
central heating 10
centre 196, 199, 201
century 198, 280
cereals 147, 157
chain-mail 24
chair 9, 18, 36, 80, 164
chalk 18, 213, 216, 306
chameleon 269
chamois leather 137
champagne 176
championship 195
change 180
changeable 259
channel 26, 187, 248, 277, 290
chapel 226
chapter 194
char 279
character 70
charge 42, 233, 296
charming 70
charred 279
chart 26
chase 30, 42, 183
chat 289
chatter 289
cheap 181
checkout 163
check-up 32
cheek 37
cheerful 50, 70
cheese 150, 155
cheetah 264
chemist 35, **82, 162**
cheque 180
chequered flag 207
cherry 146, 270
chess 185
chest 37

chestnut 311
chest of drawers 12, 164
chewing gum 159
chicane 207
chicken 148, 158
chicken pox 33
chief constable 296
children 19, 100
chilly 260
chime 285
chimney 7
chimpanzee 264
china 9
chips 145
chisel 136
chocolate 159
choir 31, 190
chop 148, 205
chorus 190
Christmas 172, 281
church 4, 219, 226
C.I.D. 296
cigarettes 85, 170
cigars 170
cinders 279
cinema 191, 219, 226
circle 22
circuit 97
circular 302
circus 192
cirrus 258
cistern 14, 94, 278
city 195, 219
civic centre 226
civil war 24
clammy 48, 260
clamour 45
clang 45
clap 189
clash 45
clasp 64
class 19, 100
classroom 16, **18**
clatter 45
clause 21
clay 28
clean 47, 71
cleaner 17, **104**
clear 43, 259
clear round 206
clerk 107, 122
clerk of the court 297
client 107
cliff 223
climb 30, 253
climbing frame 184, 186
clinic 35, 81
clip 64
cloakroom 9
clock 9, 18, 200
(the) **clock 285**
close 260
cloth 18, 104, 121
clothes 120
clothing 58, **174, 175**
cloud 223, 250, 258, 274
cloudburst 258, 274
cloudy 44, 259
clown 192
clubs 210
coach 88, 231, 242
coal 74, 133, 305
coalface 114
coalmine 133
coalplace 7
coal scuttle 9
coal train 133
coalyard 74, 133
coarse 48, 313
coarse fishing 209
coast 26
coaster 243
coastline 250
coat 58
coat-hook 9
coat-of-arms 24
cobalt 308
cobra 269
cock 262
cockatoo 266
cockle 220, 267
cockroach 268
cocoa 151
coconut-shies 193
cod 149, 267
code 292
coffee 151
coin 180
coin box 292
coke 74, 103, 113
coke (cola) 151
colander 141
cold 33, 260
cold frame 15
cold front 259
collage 27

collar 63
collar-bone 39
collection 73, 293
college 226
colliery 74, 114
colossal 301
colour 27, 106, 213, 290, **304**
column 294
comb 119
combine 222
combine harvester 142
combustion 279
comedy 189, 290
comet 214
comic 294
comma 21
common 218
commuter train 242
compact disc 168
compact disc player 188
companion 6
compartment 242
compass 221, 238, 252
complexion 68
composition 21
compost 271
compost heap 15
computer 22, 124, 139, **140**
computer operator 125
computer programmer 125
comrade 6
concave 302
conceited 70
concert 31, **190**
concert hall 219, 226
concerto 190
condensation 275
condiments 154
condolence 172
condor 266
conductor 86, 190, 234
cones 228
confectionery 153
conflagration 279
confluence 224
congratulations 172
conical 302
conifer 270
conjurer 187
connect 97
connector 167
conquer 24
conservatory 7
constable 76, 296
constellation 214
consultant 35
container 111
container lorry 235
contented 50
contents 194
continent 215
continental quilt 12
contra-flow 228
contrast 290
contributor 294
controls 88
control tower 251
convalescent 34
convent 226
conversation 289
converse 289
convex 302
conveyor 93
conveyor belt 114
cook 17, **102**
cooked 152
cooker 10
cooking 134, **141, 152**
cooking-oil 150
cool 54, 260
coot 265
co-pilot 250
copper 180, 217
copy 19
cord 66
cordless phone 292
core 146
cormorant 265
corn 147, 222
corner 196, 199, 207
corn flakes 147
correction 100
corridor 16, 242
cosmetics 162
cosmonaut 256
costume 203
cot 12
cottage 7
cotton 66
couch 9, 36, 80
cough 33
count 211

countdown 255
counter 84, 177
country 26, **218**
county 195
coupling 241
coupon 181
courage 54
courageous 54
courgette 145
course 123, 210
court 30, 108, 184, 201, 204, **297**, 303
courteous 70
cousin 2
cover 194
covered 178
cow 262
cowardly 53
cowshed 222
coxswain 246
crab 149, 220, 267
crackle 279
craft 28
crane 111, 112, 247, 266
cranefly 268
crash 45
crash helmet 236
crate 179
crater 257
cravat 63
crawl 41, 203
crayon 18, 27
creak 45
cream 72, 150, 155, 306
crease 28, 198
credit card 180
credit-card phone 292
credit note 181
creep 41
cremate 279
cremated 5
cremation 279
crematorium 5
cress 145
crew 220, **246**
cricket 198, 268
crime 299
criminal 299
Crimplene 66
crimson 307
crisp 260
crisps 145
crockery 11, 123, 154
crocodile 269
crooked 303
crops 127, 218, 222
cross 52
crossing 219
crossroads 229
crossword 294
crow 265
crowd 195
cruel 70
cruise 243
crumbling 48
crumpet 153
crunch 45
crusade 24
cuckoo 265
cucumber 145
cue 213
cuff 59
culvert 277
cumulus 258
cunning 70
cupboard 10, 18, 164
curious 56
curls 173
curly 69
currant 146
current 97, 220
curtain 8, 189
curved 302
cushion 9
custard 153
custody 296
customs 247, 251
cut 28
cutlery 11, 123, 154
cut off 292
cutter 109
cutting 106
cutting board 11
cuttings 271
cycle path 227
cycle racing 208
cyclone 258
cylinder 302
cylindrical 302

dace 267
daddy-longlegs 268
daily 284, 294
dainty 67, 300
dairy 72, **155**, 222
daisy 271

dam 277
dame 189
damp 259, 276
damson 146
dance 30, 42, 183
dandelion 271
danger 114, 135
dank 275
daring 54
dark 44, 68, **305**
Dark Ages 25
dark side (moon) 257
dart 42
dartboard 185
darts 185
dashboard 232
database 140
date 24
daughter 1
davit 244
dawdle 41
dawn 284
day 280, **283**
daybreak 284
daytime 284
dazzling 43
deadline 105
deafening 45
dear 181
death 5
debate 289, 295
decade 280
deceitful 70
December 282
deciduous 270
decimal 22
deck 117, 244
deckchair 220
declare 251
declared 198
decoration 8
decorator 96
deep 220, 224
deer 263
defence 108, 297
defend 24, 110, 196, 297
defendant 108
deformed 67, 303
dejected 51
delicate 32, 67
delicious 49
delighted 50
delightful 71
deliver 179
delivery 72, 73, 87, **179**, 293
delivery van 294
deluge 274
demand 289
denims 59
dental surgeon 36
dentist 36, 80
department store 171, 219, 226
dependable 70
deposit 179
depot 78
depressed 51
depression 259
depth 221
deputy head 17
derrick 117, 244
descend 253
descendant 1
descent 253, 254
describe 289
desert 215
design 28
desk 18, 100, 122
dessert 144
destination 87, 234
detached 7
detective 76, 187, 194, 296
dew 275
diagonal 302
dial 292
dialling 292
diamond 217
dictation 21
dictionary 194
died 5
diesel 132, 241
diet 32
dig 129
digestion 38
digger 230
digital recording 168
dim 44
diminutive 300
din 45
dinghy 243
dingo 264
dining-car 242
dining-room 9, 16
dinner 144
dinner lady 17
dipped 232

dipstick 233
direction 252
director 290
directory 292
dirt 114
dirty 71
disabled 67
disc 39, 125, 168
discharged 297
disconnected 292
discontented 52
discount 181
discouraged 51
discus 200
discuss 289
discussion 289
disease 33
disfigured 303
dish 11, 144
dishwasher 10
disinfectant 33, 104
dismal 51
dispense 82
display 84
displeased 52
distance 252
distorted 303
distressed 51
distribution 131
district nurse 81
ditch 218
divan 9
dive 203, 221
diver 272
diversion 227
divide 22
diving bell 272
divorced 4
dock 111, 116, 117, 133, 247, 297
docker 111
doctor 35, 79
document 107
documentary 290
dodge 183
dodgems 193
dog 261
dogfish 267
doll 160
doll's house 160, 185
dolphin 267
domestic animals 262
domestic tools 137
domestic water 278
dominoes 185
donkey 220, 237, 261
door 7, 92, 103
doorstep 7
double bed 12
double-decker 234
double fence 206
double-glazed 7
double-glazing 92
doubles 204
downcast 51
downhearted 51
downpour 258, 274
downspout 7
downstairs 9
downy 48
drab 71
dragonfly 268
drain 7, 277
drainer 10
drank 144
draught 272
draughts 185
draw 27
drawing-board 91
drenched 276
dress 59, 175
dressing gown 61
dressing-table 12, 164
dressmaker 121
dress shop 175
dribble 196
drier 119, 173
drift 254
drill 36, 80, 89, 98, 109, 118, 132, 136
drink 144
dripping 276
drive 210, 227
driver 78, 86, 207
drizzle 258, 274
drought 259
drown 248
dry 259
drybrush 96
dry dock 247
dry goods 157
dual carriageway 229
dubbing-mixer 290
duck 225, 265
duffel coat 58
dull 44, 71, 259
dumb 46

dummy 197
dumper 230
dune 215
dungarees 59
dungeon 24
dusk 284
dusky 68
dust cart 235
duster 18, 104, 137
dustman 75
dustpan 137
duty 247
duvet 12
dwarf 300
dye 119, 304
dynamo 131

eager 55
eagle 210, 265
ear 37
early 286
earpiece 292
ear-splitting 45
earth 15
earth track 257
earthworm 268
earwig 268
easel 160
east 26
Easter 281
easy-chair 9, 164
eat 144
eating 144
ebony 305
echo 45
edit 105, 294
edition 294
editor 105, 294
editorial 294
educational aids 20
Edwardian 25
eel 267
egg 150, 155, 222
eiderdown 12
elated 55
elbow 37
electric 10, 240, 241
electric fire 9
electrician 97
electricity 97, **131**
electrics 115, **167**
electric tools 136
electronic 200
electronics 139
elegant 71
elephant 237, 264
elephantine 301
elliptical 302
elm 270
embroider 29
emerald 217, 309
emergency 78, 292
emergency-chute 250
emergency door 250
emu 266
emulsion 95
encore 190
encyclopaedia 194
endurance 208
engaged 4, 292
engagement 172
engine 241, 279
engineer 109, 246
engine shed 240
English 21
enormous 301
enquire 289
enthusiastic 55
entrance 7, 16, 177, 228
envelope 293
epidemic 33
equator 26
equinox 281
erosion 224
erupt 215
escalator 171
essay 21
estate car 231
estimate 22
estimated time of arrival 252
estuary 224
E.T.A. 252
evaporate 275
evening 284
event 24, 200
ever 287
evergreen 270
ewe 128, 262
exact fare 86
examination 21, 79, 83, 130
examine 36, 80
excavate 129
excavator 230
exchange 292
excited 50, 55
excitement 55
exciting 191

exclaim 289
exercise 21
exercise book 20
exhaust 272
exit 177, 189, 228
expenditure 124
expensive 181
experiment 23
explain 289
explore 221
explosion 45
express 242
extensive 301
extraction 36, 80
eye 37
eyelash 37
eyelid 37

face 37
facecloth 13
factory 226
faint 44, 46
fair 68, 69, 70, **193**
fairway 210
fairy godmother 189
fairy tale 194
falcon 265
fall 42, 212
fall-pipe 7
family 1
fan 272
fare 234, 239
fare stage 234
farm 72, **142**, 218, **222**
farmhouse 127, 222
farming 127
farmyard 222
fascinated 56
fashionable 71
fast 42, 285
fasteners 64
fat 67, 143, 150
father 1
father-in-law 2
fault 204, 205, 206
fawn 311
fear 53
fearful 53
fearless 54
feather duster 137
February 282
fed-up 52
feeble 32
feet 60
fence 7, 222
fender 9
ferret 263
ferry 111, 224
fertiliser 15, 222, 271
fetid 47
feverish 32
fibreglass 14
fiction 126, 194
field 127, 184, 200, 218, 250
fielder 198
fifteen 197
fight 110
figures 22
file 122, 136
filling 36, 80
filling station 233
film 162, 191
filter 277
fin 250
finch 265
fine 259, 298, 313
finger 37, 149
finish 207
finishing-line 200
fiord 215
fir 270
fire 77, 279
fire-alarm 279
fire-blanket 77
fire-brigade 279
fire-engine 77, 235, 279
fire-extinguisher 77, 279
fire guard 77
fire hydrant 279
fireman 77, 279
fireplace 9
fire-station 77, 219, 279
firm 48
first 286
first-aid 78
first class 293
fish 149, 221
fisherman 116
fishing 209
fishing boat 220
fit 32
fitted kitchen 10
fitter 109
fitting 115, 121

flabby 48
flag 196, 210, 245
flame 279
flamingo 266
flammable 279
flan 153
flashers 78
flashing 43
flat 7, 302
flea 268
flew 250
flexible 48
flicker 279
flight 250
flight path 251
flint 170, 216, 279
flippers 221
float 72, 220
floating dock 247
flock 128
flood 94, 224, 274
floor 92, 171
floorcloth 137
floor-manager 290
floppy disc 140
florist 166
flounder 267
flour 156
flow 224
flower 15, 166, 218, 225, 271
flower-bed 271
'flu 33
fluffy 313
fluorescent 43
flush 13
fly 186, 250, 268
fly-fishing 209
flying fish 267
F.M. 291
foal 261
fodder 237
fog 258, 275
foggy 44
fog lamp 232
fold 28
folding 106
foliage 271
follow-my-leader 183
food processor 11, 141
foot 37
football 196, 272
football ground 226
footpath 238
ford 224
forecast 259
forehand 204
forehead 37
forest 215
forest fire 279
forging 113
fork 15, 138, 141, 229
fork-lift truck 111, 247
form 19
fortnight 280
fortune-teller 193
forward 196
foul 47, 196, 199, 201, 211
foul stroke 213
foundations 92
fountain 277
fox 263
fraction 22
fracture 34
fragrance 47
fragrant 47
frail 32, 67
frame 89, 213
franking 293
fraud 299
freckles 68
free-kick 196
free-style 203
free wheel 208
freeze 94
freezer 10
freezing 259, 260
freezing fog 258
freight 239
french window 7
frequency 291
frequently 287
fresh 47
friction 279
Friday 283
fridge 10
fried 152
friendly 70
friends 6
friendship 6
frightened 53
frigid 260
frog 267
frost 258
frosty 260
frozen 258, 260

frozen food 163
frozen vegetables 145
fruit 146, 271
fruit juice 151
fry 102, 152
fuel 103, 170
full 182
full stop 21
full-time 196
fume 279
funeral 5
funnel 244
furious 52
furniture 164
furrow 222
furry 313
fuse 97, 167
fuselage 250
future 286

galaxy 214
gale 258
galleria 178
galley 250
gallon 233
gallop 237
game 30, 160, 183, 204
gantry 112
gaol 298
garage 7, 219, **233**
garden 15, 16, **138**, 219, **271**
gardener 17
gargantuan 301
garlic 145
gas 10, **134**, 254
gas-cooled 135
gas fire 9
gas fitter 99
gas holder 134
gate 7, 103, 222, 225, 249
gauge 98
gaunt 67
gazelle 264
gear 207, 208, 236
geese 225
general 32, 197
generator 131
gentle 70
gentlemen 173
geography 26
gerbil 261
germ 33
get well 172
giant 301
gibbon 264
gift-wrap 182
gigantic 301
gin 176
giraffe 264
glacial 260
glacier 215
glad 50
glaring 43
glass 9, 13
glassware 123
gleaming 43
glide 272
glider 272
glittering 43
globe 20, 26
gloomy 51
gloss paint 95
glossy 43, 48
gloves 58, 174, 198, 211
glow 279
glowing 43
glue 28
gnat 268
goal 195, 201
goalkeeper 196
goalpost 196
goat 262
gold 217, 310
golden 69
golf 210
goods 84
goose 265
gooseberry 146
gorge 215
gorilla 264
gossip 289
government 295
gown 59
grades 133
gradient 223
grain silo 222
gram 22
grammar 21
grandchild 1
granddaughter 1
grandfather 1
grandmother 1
grandparents 1
grandson 1
granite 216
grape 146

graph 22
grass 15, 225, 309
grasshopper 268
grassland 215
grass snake 263, 269
grate 9
gratified 50
graving dock 247
gravy 152
graze 222
greasy 48
great 301
great circle 252
green 210, **309**
greenfly 268
greenhouse 15
greet 289
greeting 172
grey 69
grief-stricken 51
grill 10, 102
grilled 152
grinder 11
gripped 56
grizzly bear 264
groceries 150
grocery 157
groom 237
ground 198
group 19
grouse 265
grub 268
guard 88
guard's van 242
gudgeon 267
guest 4
guilty 108, 297
guinea pig 261
guitar 31
gulf 215
gull 265
gums 36
gusher 118
gust 258
gutter 7

haddock 149, 267
hail 274
hair 37, **69**
hair cream 173
haircut 173
hairdresser 119, 173
hairstyle 173
hairy 48, 313
hake 149
half-brother 1
half past 285
half-sister 1
half-term 281
half-time 196
halibut 267
hall 9, 16, 190
Halloween 281
ham 148, 158
hamburger 148
hamlet 218
hammer 89, 136, 200
hamster 261
hand 37
handlebars 236
handrail 9
handstand 30
hang 96
hangar 251
Hanoverian 25
happy 50
happy ending 189
harbour 117, 220, 247
hard 48
hard frost 259
hard hat 114, 118
hard shoulder 228
hardware 125, 140
hard water 278
hare 263
harness 237
harrow 142
harvest 127, 222
hat 62, 174
hatchback 231
hawk 265
hawser 245
hawthorn 270
hay 222
hay fever 33
haystack 222
hay whisk 142
hazel 270
hazel nut 146
head 37, **62**
header 196
headgear 208
headlights 232
headline 294
headmaster 17, 101
headmistress 17, 101
head's room 16

head teacher 17, **101**
health centre 79
health – **general 32**
healthy 32
hear 289
hearing 45, 46
heart 38
heartbroken 51
hearth 9
heath 218
heating 103, 134
heats 200
heat shield 257
heat wave 259
hedge 7, 218, 222, 271
hedge-clipper 138
hedgehog 263
heifer 262
height 223, 253
helicopter 250, 272
heli-pad 118
helmet 24, 76, 77
help 100
helper 6
helpful 177
helter-skelter 193
hem 29
hen 262
heroic 54
heron 265
herring 149, 267
hexagonal 302
hide-and-seek 183
hi-fi 168, 188
high 259
high-fidelity 168
high-jump 200
high tea 144
hike 238
hill 26, 218
hill-climb 208
hinge 115
hip 39
hippopotamus 264
hire-purchase 180
historical 194
historical periods 25
history 24
hit 184
hob 10
hobble 41
hockey 199
hockey stick 199
hod 93
hoe 15, 138
hog 262
hold 117, 212, 244
hole 210
holiday 19, 281
holly 270
home 196
home computer 9
homework 100
homicide 299
honest 70
honey 150
honeymoon 4
hood 62
hook 209
hook-and-eye 64
hoop 192
hop 30, 41
hopper 133
horizon 244
horizontal 302
hornbill 266
hornet 268
horrified 53
horse 24, 192, 237, 261
horse chestnut 270
hose 77, 278
hosepipe 15, 138
hospital 34, 78, 81, 219, 226
hot 49, 260
hot air 254
hotel 219, 226
hot plate 10
hour 280
house 7, 8
houseboat 249
housecoat 61
House of Commons 295
House of Lords 295
hovercraft 243, 272
hovermower 15
how often? 287
how soon? 288
H.P. 180
hue 304
huge 301
hull 112
humid 259, 260, 275
humidity 259, 275
humming bird 266
humorous 70
hurdles 200

hurricane 258
hurry 42
hurtle 42
husband 1
hushed 46
hut 16
hydrant 77, 277
hydrogen 273
hyena 264

ice 258, 274
iceberg 215
ice cap 215
ice cream 153
icefield 215
ice-skates 186
icicle 258, 274
icy 260
ignite 279
ignition 279
iguana 269
ill 32
illness 33
illustration 20, 194
immeasurable 301
immediately 288
immense 301
immersion heater 14
immunise 33
imprisonment 298
inaudible 46
incinerate 279
income 124
indented 313
index 194
indigo 308
indistinct 44
indoors 185
industries 26
inexpensive 181
infinite 301
infinitesimal 300
inflate 250, 254, 272
influenza 33
inform 289
information 194
infrequently 287
ingot 113
injection 33, 35, 36, 80
injury 299
ink 18, 106
innings 184, 198
innocent 108, 297
insects 218
insert 292
insipid 49
inspector 76, 239, 296
inspired 55
instantly 288
instep 37
instrument 31, 190
insulation 14
inter-city 242
interest 56
interested 56
interface 140
international 195, 292
interval 189
interview 101
interview-room 296
intestine 38
invertebrates 268
invisible 44
invitation 4
iris 37
iron 210, 217
ironmonger 165
irregular 303
irritated 52
island 26, 215
isobar 259
isthmus 215
ivory 306

jackal 264
jackdaw 265
jacket 58, 174, 194
jade 309
jagged 48, 313
jaguar 264
jail 298
jam 150
January 282
jar 82, 157
javelin 200
jaw 39
jay 265
jealous 70
jeans 59
jelly 153
jersey 59, 208
jet 277, 278, 305
jet engine 250
jetty 247
jigsaw 185
join 99
joiner 89

joint 37, 89, 99
journal 294
journalist 105, 294
journey 88
joyful 50
judge 108, 297
jug 141
juggernaut 235
juggler 192
juicy 146
July 282
jump 30, 42, 183
jumper 59, 174, 175, 206
jump-off 206
junction 228
June 282
jungle 215
jury 108, 297

kangaroo 264
keel 112
keen 260
kerosene 132
kestrel 265
kettle 11, 141
key 103
kid 262
kidney 38, 148, 158
kilogram 22
kilometre 22, 252
kilt 59
kind 70
kindle 279
king 24
kingfisher 265
kiosk 292
kipper 149
kiss-of-life 34
kitchen 10, 16, 102
kite 186, 272
kitten 261
kiwi 266
kiwi-fruit 146
knee 37
kneecap 39
knickers 61
knife 28, 141
knitting 29
knob 7
knockdown 211
knocker 7
knockout 211, 212
knot 252
knuckle 37
koala bear 264
kookaburra 266

labourer 129
laburnum 270
laces 64
lackadaisical 57
ladder 77, 95, 103
ladies 173
ladybird 268
lager 176
lagging 14
lake 26, 218, 225, 273
lamb 128, 148, 158, 262
lamp 8
landing 254
landing-stage 247
landing wheels 250
lane 200, 203, 218, 227
language 289
lanky 67
lap 200, 207
lard 150
larder 10
large 301
lark 265
last 286
last week 283
late 286
later 288
lathe 109
launch 112, 243, 255
launching pad 255
lava 215
law-making 295
lawn 15, 271
lawnmower 15, 138
lawyer 107
layby 229
lead 217
leaf 309
league 195, 197
leak 94, 99
lean 40, 67
lean-to 15
leap 42
leap-frog 183
leap year 280
learning 130
leaves 271
ledger 122
leek 145
left-luggage 239

leg 37
leg-warmers 58
lemon 146, 310
lending library 126
lens 23, 37
leopard 264
less gravity 257
lesson 19
let 204
letter 73, 161, **293**, 294
letter box 7
lettuce 145
level 90, 302
level-crossing 88, 229, 240
librarian 126
library 16, 194, 219, 226
lice 268
licence 161
licence disc 232
lid 18
lie 40
lifebelt 248
lifeboat 243
life-cord 256
lifejacket 245, 250
lift 171
lift-off 255
light 8, 189, **306**
lighter 170, 279
lighthouse 248
lighting 120
lightning 258
lightship 243
lilac 312
lime 270
limestone 216
limousine 231
limp 41
line 209
line-judge 204
line-out 197
liner 243
linesman 196
linger 41
lingerie 175
lino 8
lion 264
lip 37
listen 289
listless 57
litre 22, 233
litter 75
liver 38, 148, 158
lizard 269
llama 237, 264
load 87, 111
loading 247
loaf 150, 156
loaves 150, 156
lob 204, 205
lobby 9
lobster 149, 267
local 294
local train 242
lock 103, 249, 273
lock-keeper 249
locomotive 88, **241**
loft 14
lofty 301
loiter 41
long-distance 292
long-jump 200
long wave 291
loofah 13
lorry 87, 231, 235
lotion 35
loud 45
lounge 9, 40
louse 268
loving 70
low 259
L.P. 168, 188
lubricating 132
ludo 185
luggage 239
lull 46
luminous 43
lumpy 48
lunar expedition 257
lunch 144
lung 38, 272
lurch 41
luscious 49
lyre bird 266

macaroni 147
macaw 266
machine 106, 109
machinery 127
mackerel 149, 267
mackintosh 58
magazine 85, 105, 120, 294
magenta 307
maggot 268
magician 187
magistrate 108, 297

magnet 23
magnifier 23
magpie 265
mail van 73, 293
main 277
main beam 232
main course 144
main road 227
mallet 136
mamba 269
mammoth 301
manager 177, 196
mango 145
manslaughter 299
mantelpiece 9
manure 15, 222, 271
map 26, 90
marathon 200
marbles 185
March 282
march 42
margarine 150
marine 110
mark 21
market 178, 219, 226
marking 100
maroon 307
marriage 4
married 4
marrow 145
marsh 218
martin 265
mashed 152
mask 221
massive 301
mast 245, 290
mat 8, 164
match 96, 170, 195, 204, 279
mate 6
material 29, **66**
mathematics 22
matinee coat 65
matron 81
mattress 12
mauve 312
May 282
meadow 218
meal 87, 102, **144**
mealie flour 147
mean 70
meander 224
measles 33
measure 23
measurement 22, 90, **280**
measuring 90
meat 148, 158
meat pie 158
mechanic 98, 109
medal 195
medicine 35, 82, 162
medium wave 291
meeting 200
melon 146
melt 279
menagerie 192
mention 289
menu 123, 154
metal 113
meteor 214
meteorite 214
meteorological office 259
meteorology 259
meter 97, 99
metre 22
microscopic 300
microwave 10
midday 284
midget 300
midnight 284
midsummer 281
midwife 81
mighty 301
mild 49, 259
mile 252
military 110
milk 72, 150, 155
milk-cooler 222
milk race 208
milk shake 151
millisecond 280
mime 190
mince 148
minced 152
minced beef 148, 158
mine 114
miner 74, **114**
minerals 143, 151, **217**
miniature 300
minnow 267
minor 300
mint 145
minuscule 300
minute 280, 300
mirage 215

mirror 9, 12, 13
miscue 213
miserable 51
mis-shapen 303
mission control 255
mist 223, 258, **275**
misty 44
mittens 58, 65
mixer 141
mixer tap 10
mobile 27
mobile home 7
model 28, 91, **120**, 160
modern 25, 286
module 257
moist 276
molars 36
mole 263
molten 113
molten rock 215
moment 285
monastery 226
Monday 283
money 84, 180, 292
monkey 264
mono 168
Monopoly 185
monsoon 258
monstrous 301
month 280
monument 226
moon 214
moon-dust 257
moon-landing 257
moon-mobile 257
moon-orbit 257
moon-rock 257
moon-track 257
moor 218
moorhen 265
moose 264
mop 104, 137
morning 284
mortar 93
mosquito 268
moth 268
mother 1
mother-in-law 2
motorbike 236
motor boat 243
motorcyclist 236
motor launch 249
motor-racing 207
motorway 228
mountain 26, 215, 218, **223**
mournful 51
mousey 69
moustache 69
mouth 37, 224
mouthpiece 292
movements 41, 42
movie 191
mower 142
mud 221
mudguards 236
muffin 153
muffler 63
mule 237
multiple 115
multiply 22
mumps 33
murder 299
muscle 37
muscular 67
museum 219, 226
music 31
musical 187, 290
music centre 9, 291
music room 16
mussel 220, 267
mustard 150
musty 47
mute 46
mutilated 303
mutton 148
mynah 266
mystery 187, 194

nail 37, 89, 136, 165
nailbrush 13
nappy 65
narrowboat 249
national 195, 294
navigate 244, 252
navigator 246, 250
navy 308
neat 71
neck 37, **63**
nectarine 146
needle 29, 33
needlework 29
neighbour 6
nephew 2
net 8, 116, 184, 201, 204, 209, 220
netball 201
never 287
new baby 172

new ball 198
news 105, 290, 294
newsagent **85**, 294
newspaper 85, 105, **294**
newsreader 290
newt 267
New Year 281
next week 283
nickel 217
niece 2
night 284
nightdress 61
nil 196
nimbus 258
nitrogen 272
noise 45
noiseless 46
non-drip 95
non-fiction 126, 194
non-flammable 279
non-smoking 242
noon 284
Norman 25
north 26
North Sea 134
nose 37, 250
nostril 37
notebook 122
notes 31, 194
not out 198
nova 214
novel 194
November 282
now 286
nuclear power **135**
numb 36, 80
number 22, 196, 208, 234, 292
number plate 232
nurse 34, **81**
nut 115, 136
nutrition **143**
nylon 66

oak 270
oasis 215
oath 108
oats 147
obliging 177
observatory 214
observe 23
obsolete 286
occasionally 287
ocean 26, 215, 248, 273
o'clock 285
octagonal 302
October 282
octopus 267
odour 47
offensive 47
offer 181
office 91, 101, 107, 122, 219, 226
officer 246
off-licence 176
oil 10, 103, **132**, 233
oil-driller **118**
oil rig 118
oilskins 116, 117
oil tanker 243
oily 48
ointment 35, 82, 162
okra 145
old 24
older 19
old-fashioned 286
olive 309
Olympics 195
omelette 152
one-man bus 86
on-stream 118
opaque 44
open 178
opening hours 177
opera 190, 290
operation 34, 83
opponents 195
opposition 295
oppressive 260
orange 146, 310
orang-utan 264
orbit 214, 255
orchard 222, 271
orchestra 31, 190
order 123, 154, 179, 289
ore 113
organ **38**, 190
ornament 9
ostrich 266
otter 224, 263
out 198
outdoors **186**
outer clothing **58**
out-of-date 286
oval 302
ovation 190
oven 10, 102
over 198

overalls 58
overcast 259
overcoat 58, 174
overflow 94, 278
overpass 228
overpowering 47
overseas 264, 266, 292
owl 265
ox 237
oxbow-lake 224
oxygen 34, 78, 250, 272, 273
oxygen bottle 221
oyster 149, 267
ozone layer 258

pack 155
package 182
packet 157, 159, 170, 182
paddle 220
paddles 249
paddling pool 15, 186
paddock 222
pads 198
page 194
paid 180
paint 27, 304
painter 95
painting set 160
pair 60
palace 226
palatable 49
pale 68
palm 37
pampas 215
pan 11, 165
panda 264
panorama 223
pantograph 241
pantomime 189
pantry 10
pants 61, 174
paper 13, 27, 28, 106, 182, 293
paperback 194
paper bag 171
paper-round 294
par 210
parachute 257, 272
parade 192
paraffin 132
paragraph 21
parakeet 266
parcel 73, 161, 179, 182
parched 260
parents 1, 17
park 184, 219, **225**
parking 219
parliament 24, 295
parrot 261, 266
parsley 145
parsnip 145
partner 6
partridge 265
parts (vehicle) 232
party 4
pass 201, 215, 223
passage 9
passport 247, 251
past 24, 286
paste 28, 96, 149
pastel 27
pastille 159
pastry 152
path 7, 92, 225, 271
patient 34
patio 7
patio door 7
pattern 27, 96, 121
pavement 7, 219
pay 180
pay-as-you-enter 86, 234
pay-phone 292
P.E. 30
pea 145
peaceful 46
peach 146
peacock 265
peak 223
peanut 146
pear 146, 270
pearl 306
peat 15
pebble 220
pedal 236
pedestrian 238
pedestrian-crossing 229
pedestrian precinct 178
peel 146
pelican 266
pelican-crossing 229
pelvis 39
pen 18
penalty 196, 197

pence 180
pencil 18, 27
penguin 266
peninsula 215
pension 161
pepper 150
perch 267
perennial 271
perform 192
perfume 47, 162
period 19, 285
perm 173
permafrost 215
permanent wave 119
personal best 200
perspective drawing 91
pet 83, **261**
petite 300
petrol 132, 233
petrol pump 233
pheasant 265
photocopier 122, 139
photograph 9, 120, 294
photographer 294
phrase 21
physical education (P.E.) 30
pianist 31, 190
piano 9, 31
pick 129
pickles 150
picnic 220
picture 9, 20, 187, 194, 290
pie 153, 156
pier 220, 247
pig 262
pigeon 265
piglet 262
pigment 304
pigsty 222
pike 267
pilchard 267
pill 35, 82, 162
pillar box 73, 293
pillow 12
pilot 244, 246
pin 29
pincers 136
pine 270
pineapple 146
pink 307
pip 146
pipe 14, 94, 99, 118, 132, 170, 277
pipe-cleaner 170
pipeline 134
pips 292
pit 74, 114, 200
pitch 30, 184, 195, 198, 202, 305
pithead 114, 133
pits 207
pit stop 207
pixel 140
place-mat 9
plaice 149, 267
plain 29, 215, 218
plaited 69
plan 90, 91
plane 136, 270, 302
planet 214
planet Earth 215
plant 15, 166, 213, 222, 271
Plantagenet 25
plaster cast 34
Plasticine 28
plate 112
platform 118, 239
platinum 217
play 21, 31, **183**, 189, 194, 290
player 190, 195
playground 16, 225
playing field 16, 30
playmate 6
pleasant 70
pleased 50
pleasure 50
pliable 48
pliers 136
plimsolls 30, 60
plod 41
plough 142, 222
ploughing 127
plucky 54
plug 97, 167
plum 146, 270
plumber 94
plumbline 96
plump 67
plutonium 135
pneumatic tyre 272
poached 152

pocket 58, 180, 213
poem 21
poetry 194
points 197, 211, 213, 240
poker 9
polar bear 264
pole 26, 90, 206
pole-vault 200
police 34, 76, **296**
police car 235
policeman 219, 296
police station 76, 219, 296
policewoman 76, 296
polished 48
polishing 115
polite 177
polyester 66
pond 218, 273
pony 237, 261
pony trek 237
pool 203, 273
pop 151
pop group 187
poplar 270
porch 7
pork 148, 158
porous 313
porpoise 267
port 116, 117, 176, 244, **247**
portable 291
porter 239
porthole 244
pose 120
position 40
post 73, 202
postbox 73, 293
post code 293
postmark 293
post office 73, **161**, 226
pot 11, 141, 165, 166, 213
potato 145
potato-digger 142
pouch 170
poultry 127, 222
pound 180
powder 162
powerboat 243
powerful 67
power hammer 113
power station 131, 133
practice 130
practising 130
prairie 215
pram 186
prawn 149
praying mantis 268
prehistoric 24, 25
prepare 102
prescription 35, 79, 82, 162
present 286
preserves 157
pressing 121
press-stud 64
pressure 232
pressure-gauge 221
price 181
prickly 48, 313
primer 95
primrose 310
prince 24
principal boy 189
printer 106
print-out 125, 139
prison 108
prisoner 108, 297
prize 193
probation 298
prodigious 301
producer 290
products 26
professional 195
program 125, 139, 140
programme 187, 189, 290
programmer 168
promenade 220
promptly 288
proofs 106
propeller 244
proportionate 302
prosecute 297
prosecution 108, 297
protein 143
proud 70
provincial 294
prune 146
publisher 105
pudding 144
puff adder 269
puffin 265
pulley 245

pullover 59
pulsar 214
pumping station 277
pumps 30, 60
Punch and Judy 220
punctually 288
punctuation 21
pungent 47
punishment 298
punt 249
puny 67, 300
pupil 19, 37
puppet 187
puppy 261
purchase 180, 181
purchasing 180
purity 277
purl 29
purple 312
purse 180
pursuit 208
putt 210
puzzle 160, 185
pygmy 300
pyjamas 61
pylon 131
pyramid 302
python 269

quail 265
qualify 130
quarrelsome 70
quarter past 285
quarter to 285
quasar 214
quay 220, 247
queen 24
quench 278
question 21, 289
queue 177
quickly 288
quiet 46
quiz 187
quoits 185

rabbit 148, 261, 263
R.A.C. 232
race 183
racing car 231
rack 18
racket 184, 204
racquet 204
radar 116, 117, 251, 253
radiant 43
radiation 135
radiator 8, 10, 232, 278
radio 9, 20, 76, 87, 232, 253, **291**
radio phone 292
radio shack 244
Radio Times 187
radio tuner 168
radish 145
raft 243
rail 239, 240
rail bus 241
railway 133, 219
railway journey 240
railway station 226, 239
rain 258, **274**
rainbow 258
raincoat 58
rain gauge 259
raisin 146
rake 15, 138
ram 128, 262
range 215, 223
rank 47
rapidly 288
rapids 224
raspberry 146
rat 263
rattlesnake 269
ravine 215
raw 260
raw materials 26
reactor 135
readable 43
reading 19
reaping 127
rear light 232
receipt 171, 180, 181
receiver 291
reception 4
recline 40
reclining seat 250
record 195, 200
recorded delivery 293
recorder 31, 168
record-player 20, 168, 188
recovery 257
rectangle 22, 302
rectangular 302
red 307
reds 213

reduced 181
red wine 176
reef 221
reek 47
reel 209
re-entry 257
referee 195, 211, 212
reference 126, 194
refinery 132
reflection 43
reflector 214
refrigerator 10
refund 181
refuse 75
refuse tip 75
refuse truck 75
register 19
registered post 293
registry office 4
regular 302
regularly 287
rein 237
reindeer 264
relate 289
relation 2
relatives 2
release 296
reliable 70
remand 297
remote control 169, 187
rental 169
repair 99
reply 293
report 21, 294
reporter 105, 294
reptile 269
republic 24
request 289
reserved 70
reservoir 277
resound 45
rest 87
restaurant 219
result 23
retina 37
retirement 172
retro-rocket 257
return 204, 205
reverse-charge call 292
reversing light 232
review 294
rhinoceros 264
rib 29, 39
ribbon 64
ribcage 39
rice 147
rice crispies 147
rich 49
ride 193
ridge 223
rifle shoot 193
rig 132
ring 4, 7, 45, 211, 292
ring-master 192
river 26, 218, **224**, 273
rivet 112
rivulet 223
roach 267
road 219, **227**
road – **features 229**
road – **repairs** 103, 228, **230**
roadroller 230
roadtanker 235
roadworks 230
roar 45
roast 102, 152
robin 265
robust 32, 67
rock 216, 221, 223, 224, 248, 257
rockery 271
rocket 255
rocking-chair 164
rock pool 220
rod 209
roller 142
roller skates 186
rolling-pin 141
rolling stock 242
roll-off 111
roll-on 111
Roman 25
romp 42
roof 7, 92
rook 265
rope 30, 117, 183, 245
ropes 211, 212
rose 307
rosé (wine) 176
rostrum camera 290
rotate 214
rotavator 138
rotor 250
rouge 307

rough 48, 248, 313
round 302
roundabout 184, 193, 229
rounders 202
rounds 211
roundsman 72
roustabout 118
route 86, 87, 238, **252**
rowing boat 243
royal assent 295
rubber 18
rubbish 75, 271
ruby 217, 307
rucksack 238
rudder 244
ruddy 68, 307
rug 8, 164, 220
rugby football 197
rugged 303
ruler 18, 22
rumble 45
run 30, 42, 183, 198
running 183
run out 198
run-up 198
runway 251
rush 42, 224
russet 307
rust 311
rye 147

sack 74
sad 51
saddle 236
sadness 51
safety-net 192
saffron 310
sage 145, 309
sago 147
sail 220, 245
sailor 110
salad 145
salamander 267
salami 148
sale 181
sallow 68
salmon 149, 267
salmon ladder 224
saloon 231
salt 150, 220
salty 49
sand 200, 215, 221
sandals 60
sandbank 248
sandcastle 220
sandpit 15
sandstone 216
sandwich 152
sapphire 217, 308
sardine 149, 267
satellite-launching 256
satellite phone 292
satisfied 50
satsuma 146
saturated 276
Saturday 283
sauce 150, 154
saunter 41
sausage 148, 158
savings bank 161
savoury 49
saw 89, 136
Saxon 25
say 289
scale 26
scales 74, 141, 161, 177
scalp 37
scamper 42
scampi 149
scared 53
scarf 63
scarlet 307
scene 27
scenery 189
scent 162
scented 47
school 226
school book 194
school office 16
science 23
science fiction 187, 194
scientist 23
scissors 28, 96, 119, 121, 141
scone 153
scooter 186
scorch 279
scorching 260
score 28, 195
scrambled 152
scrapbook 160
scraper 95
scree 223
screen 125, 133
screen size 169

screw 89, 115, 136, 165, 244
screwdriver 89, 115, 136
scrum 197
scullery 10
sculpture 27
scurry 42
sea 26, 116, 215, **248**, 273
seal 263
seam 29, 114
seaman 117, 246
seaport 26
searing 260
seasick 248
seaside 220
season 281
seat 13, 18, 250
seat belt 232, 250
seaweed 220, 221
secateurs 138
second 280
second class 293
seconds 211
secretary 17, **122**
security check 251
seed 222, 271
seeder 142
seedling 271
seldom 287
selfish 70
self-service 84, 154, 233
semi-circular 302
semi-detached 7
sentence 21, 108, 297
separated 4
September 282
septic 33
serf 24
sergeant 76, 296
serial 187, 290
serrated 313
serve 177, 205
service 4, 84, 154, 204
service area 228
session 285
set 119, 187, 204
settee 9, 164
setting 106
sew 29
sewer 277
sewing-machine 29, 121
shabby 71
shade 225, 304
shadow 27
shady 44
shaft 114
shale 216
shallow 220, 224
shamble 41
shampoo 13, 119, 173
shape 22, **302, 303**
shapeless 303
shapely 302
shark 267
sharp 48, 49, 260, 313
shawl 63, 65
shearing 128
shears 138
sheep 128, 222, 223, 262
sheepdog 128
sheet 12
sheet music 31
shelf 9, 18
shell 220
shelves 9, 126, 163, 177
shepherd 128
sherry 176
shin-bone 39
shiny 43
ship 111, 117, **244**
shipbuilder 112
shipyard 112, 247
shirt 59, 196
shoal 116, 221
shock 97
shoes 60
shooter 199, 201
shop 84, 177, 178, 219
shopping list 180
shopping precinct 219
shore 220
short 67
shorthand 122
shorts 30, 59, 196
short wave 291
shot 210
shot-put 200
shoulder 37
shoulder-blade 39

shout 289
shovel 129
shower 13, 258, 274
show-jumping 206
shrimp 149, 220, 267
shrub 15, 225
shrunken 300
shuffle 41
shunting 241
shuttle 255
shuttle-landing 257
shy 70
sick 32
sickly 49
side 184
sideboard 9
sideboards 69
sideburns 69
siding 88, 240
siege 24
sieve 141
sight 43, 44
sighting 90
signal 88, 240
signal box 240
silage 222
silence 46
silk 66
silkworm 268
silo 142
silt 224
silver 180, 217, 306
sincere 70
singe 279
singing 31
single 168, 188
single bed 12
single-decker 234
single parent 1
singles 204
singlet 61
sink 10, 18
siren 77, 78, 235, 279
sister 1, 81
sister-in-law 2
sit 40
sitting room 9
size 300, 301
skate 267
skateboard 186
skeleton 39
sketch 27
skin 146
skin-diver 221
skip 42, 183
skipper 246
skipping rope 160
skirt 59, 175
skirting board 8
skittles 185
skull 39
sky 308
skyscraper 219, 226
slacks 59
slam 45
slate 7, 216
sleeper 240
sleeping-car 242
sleet 258, 274
sleeve 59, 168
slender 67
slice 141, 204
slide 184
slim 67
slimy 48
slippers 60
slippery 48
slipway 112
slither 41
slope 223
slow 41, 285
slow-worm 269
sly 70
small 67
smart 71
smash 204, 205
smell 47, 99
smelly 47
smock 59
smog 258
smoke 279
smokeless fuel 74
smoke-stack 244
smooth 48, 313
smooth snake 269
smoulder 279
snack 144
snack bar 219
snap 185
snooker 213
snorkel 221, 272
snow 258, 274, 306
soaked 276
soap 13, 104
soar 272
soccer 196
socket 97
socks 59, 174
sofa 9
sofa-bed 164
soft 48

softening 277
software 125, 140
soft water 278
soil 15
solar panel 256
solar system 214
soldering iron 136
soldier 110, 160, 185
sole 149, 267
solicitor 107
solid 48
solid fuel 10
solo 31
soloist 190
solstice 281
sombre 305
somersault 30, 192
some time 288
sometimes 287
son 1
soot 305
sorrowful 51
sorry 51
sorting office 73
sound 290
soundless 46
soundproof 46
sound-recorder 290
soundtrack 191
sour 49
source 224
south 26
sow 262
space docking 256
space laboratory 256
spacesuit 256
space transport 255
space walk 256
spade 15, 129, 138, 220
spaghetti 147
spanner 98, 115, 136
spare parts 233
spark 97, 279
sparkling 43, 176
sparrow 265
(in) spate 224
speak 289
speaker 188, 291, 295
special effects 191
specialist 35
spectator 195
speech 289
speedboat 243
speedily 288
speedometer 232
spelling 21
sphere 302
spherical 302
spicy 49
spider 268
spiky 313
spin 198
spinach 145
spine 39
spinnaker 245
spinster 4
spiral 302
spirit-level 93
splash 45, 220
splashdown 257
sponge 13, 104, 153, 208
spoon 141
sport 194, 294
sport – **general 197**
sports car 231
sprat 267
sprawl 40
spray 15, 166, 222, 278
spraying 115
spreader 230
spring 42, 223, 224, 281
springy 48
sprint 42, 200, 208
sprouts 145
square 22, 302
squash 151
squat 40
squid 267
squirrel 263
stable 237
stacker 142
stadium 200, 226
staff nurse 81
staffroom 16
stag 263
stage 189
stagger 41
stairs 9, 16, 92
stale 49
stall 178, 193
stamp 73, 161, 181, 293
stand 40
star 191, 213

starboard 244
starfish 220
starling 265
starting grid 207
starting gun 200
statement 296
station 88, 219, 290
stationmaster 239
S.T.D. 292
steak 148
steam 241, 275
steaming 260
steel 112
steelworker 113
steeplechase 200
steer 236, 244
steering wheel 232
stench 47
step-daughter 1
steppe 215
stepping-stones 224
steps 16
stepson 1
stereo 9, 168, 232, 291
stern 70, 244
stethoscope 35, 79
steward 250
stewardess 250
stewed 152
stick 28, 182
stick insect 268
stickleback 267
sticky 48
stink 47
stirrup 237
stitch 29
stock 84, 179, 222
stockings 59, 175
stomach 38
stomach-ache 33
stone 7
stool 10, 164, 209
stop 86
stopcock 278
stopping train 242
stop press 294
stop watch 200
storage 14
stork 266
storm 116, 117, 258
stormy 259
story 21, 194
stove 10, 102
straight 69, 207, 302
strait 215
stratosphere 258, 272
straw 222
strawberry 146
stream 218, 224, 273
street 219, 227
stretcher 34, 78
stride 42
strike 209
striker 196
string 28
stringline 93
strip 196
stroll 41
strong 32, 49, 67
Stuart 25
stubborn 70
studio 290
study 130
stuffy 47
stumble 41
stumped 198
stumps 198
stunted 300
sturdy 67
style 91, 119
submission 212
substitute 196
subtract 22
suction 272
suddenly 288
suffocating 47
sugar 150
suggest 289
suit 58, 174
suite 164
sultry 260
sum 22
summer 281
summit 223
summons 297
sun 214
sunburnt 68, 220
Sunday 283, 294
sunny 259
sunrise 284
sunset 284
superintendent 76, 296
supermarket 163
supervisor 17, 177
supper 144
supply 179
supporter 6, 195
surf 220

surface 221
surface mail 295
surgeon 34
surgery 35, 36, 79, 80, 83
surveyor 90
swallow 265
swamp 215
swan 225, 265
swarthy 68
sweat 275
sweater 59, 175
sweating 260
swede 145
sweet 47, 49, 144
sweet chestnut 270
sweets 85, 159
sweetshop 159
sweltering 260
swift 265
swiftly 288
swim 220, 221
swimming 203
swimming pool 16, 226
swimsuit 59
swing 15, 183, 184, 225
swing bridge 249
switch 8, 97, 167, 187
swordfish 267
sycamore 270
symmetrical 302
sympathetic 56, 70
symphony 190
synagogue 226
syrup 150

table 9, 18, 96, 123, 154, 213
tablecloth 9, 123
tables 22
tablet 35, 82, 162
table-tennis 185, **205**
tachograph 87, 235
tack 29
tackle 196, 197, 237
tadpole 267
tail 250
tailback 229
tailboard 235
tailor 121, 174
take-away 144
take-off 200
talk 289
tall 67
tallboy 12, 164
tan 311
tang 47
tangerine 146
tangled 69
tank 233, 278
tanker 72, 132
tanned 68
tap 10, 18, 94, 278
tape 182
tape measure 121
tape recorder 20, 168, 188
tapioca 147
tarantula 268
tarmac 230
tart 49, 153, 156
taste 49
tasteless 49
tasty 49
tattered 71
tax 124
taxi 231
taxi-rank 239
tea 144, 151
teacher 17, **100**
team 19, 30, 184, 195
team-mate 6
team tag 212
tee 210
teeth 36, 37, 80
telephone 9, **292**
telephone exchange 226
telescope 214
teletext 169
television 9, 20, **169, 187, 290**
tell 289
temperate 259, 260
temperature 33, 259, **260**
temple 37, 226
tench 267
tennis 204
tent 186, 193
term 19, 281
terminal 140, 251
terminus 234, 239
terrace 7
terrapin 267
terrified 53

Terylene 66
test 21, 23
testing 115
textbook 20, 194
texture 313
thatch 7
theatre 34, **189**, 219, 226
theft 299
then 286
theodolite 90
thermometer 23, 33, 259
thermostat 10
thick 48
thickset 67
thief 299
thieves 299
thigh-bone 39
thin 48, 67
thirteen 197
this afternoon 283
this evening 283
this morning 283
this week 283
thread 29
three-piece suite 9
thrilled 55
thrush 265
thumb 37
thunder 45, 258
Thursday 283
ticket 86, 234, 239
ticket-collector 88, 239
tide 220, 248, 273
tie 63, 174
tie-pin 63
tie-up 245
tiger 264
tightrope 192
tights 59, 175
tile 7, 8
till 84, 163, 180
tiller 245
time 24
time fault 206
time keeper 211
timetable 19, 285
timid 53
timing 200
tin 157, 217
tinge 304
tint 119, 304
tiny 67, 300
tip 154, 213
tired 57
tit 265
title 194
T-junction 31, 229
toad 267
toasted 152
toaster 11, 141
tobacco 85, 170
tobacconist 170
today 283
toddle 41
toe 37
toffee 159
toggle 64
toilet 13, 94
toilet articles 162
token 86
tomato 145, 146
tomorrow 283
tone 292, 304
tongs 9
tongue 37, 148
tonight 283
tonne 22
tonsilitis 33
tool 165
toolshed 15
toothbrush 13
toothpaste 13
topaz 310
topple 41
top spin 205
torch 221
tornado 258
torrent 224
torrid 260
tortoise 261, 269
totter 41
toucan 266
touch 48, 197, 203
touch-down 257
tousled 69
towel 13
towering 301
town 219, 250
town hall 226
towpath 249
toyshop 160
trace element 143
track 200, 240
tractor 142, 222
traffic 219
traffic jam 229
traffic lights 229
tragedy 189

trailer 235
train 88
trainer 196
trainers 60
training 130
train set 160
tranquil 46
transistor 291
transparent 43
transport 26
transport café 87
trapeze artist 192
trawl 116
tray 11, 123, 154
tread 232
treatment 35, 79, 83
tree 218, 225, **270**
tremendous 301
trial 297
triangle 22, 302
triangular 302
tributary 224
tricycle 186
trifling 300
trim 67, 173
triple fence 206
trolley 9, 163, 182
tropical 260
trot 42, 237
trough 222
trousers 59, 174, 175
trout 267
trowel 93, 138
truck 87, 235, 242
trudge 41
truncheon 76
trunk 37
trunk and legs 59
trunk road 227
trunks 59
truthful 70
try 197
T-shirt 59
tube 159
Tudor 25
Tuesday 283
tumble-drier 10
tuna 149, 267
tundra 215
tuner 188, 291
tunic 58
tuning 291
tunnel 240, 249
turban 62
turbine 131
turbulence 250
turkey 148, 158
turn 184
turned-on 55
turnip 145
turntable 77, 240
turquoise 308
turtle 267
TV aerial 7
TV set 169
TV Times 187
tweed 66
twenty-four hour clock 285
twilight 284
twin 1
twinkling 43
twist 192
twisted 303
type 106
typewriter 122
typhoon 258
typing 293
typist 122
tyre 232

ultramarine 308
umpire 195, 204, 213
uncle 2
unconscious 34
undercarriage 250
undercoat 95
underpass 228
undersized 300
underwater 221
underwear 61, 175
uneasy 53
uneven 48
ungrateful 70
unhappy 51
unhealthy 32
uniform 76, 123
uninterested 57
union 197
unit 10
universe 214
university 226
unkempt 71
unkind 70
unlit 44
unload 111
unloading 247
unmanned station 88
unpleasant 70

unreadable 44
unselfish 70
unsettled 259
untidy 71
unwell 32
upright 302
uproar 45
uranium 135
usherette 191
utensil 11, 165
utility room 9

vaccination 33
vacuum 272
vacuum cleaner 104, 137
valiant 54
valley 215, 218
van 87, 179, 235
vapour 275
variety show 187
vase 9, 166
vast 301
V.A.T. 180
vault 30
veal 148, 158
vegetable 15, **145**, 222, 271
vehicle 231
vehicle – **parts 232**
vein 38
Velcro 64
velvet 66
velvety 48
ventilation 272
veranda 7
verdict 108, 297
vermilion 307
vertebrae 39
vertical 302
vest 30, 61, 174
vet 83, 261
veterinary surgeon 83, 261
vexed 52
V.H.F. 291
viaduct 240
vice 136
Victorian 25
video 9, 290
video cassette 169
video recorder 20, 169, 188
videotape 188
view 223, 250
vigorous 32
village 218
villain 189
vinegar 150
violet 312
violin 30
viper 269
virus 33
visibility 259
visible 43
visitor 34
vitamin 143
voice 31
volcano 215
vole 224
volley 204
volume 194
voluminous 301
vulture 266
waddle 41
wader 209
wagon 133, 242
wagtail 265
waistcoat 58
waiting-room 79
waitress 123, 154
walk 238
wall 7, 92, 206
wallaby 264
wall bars 30
wall chart 20
wallet 180
wall map 20
wallpaper 8, 96
walnut 146, 270
war 110
ward 34
warden 219
wardrobe 12, 164
warehouse 111
warm 260
warm front 259
warn 289
wash basin 13
washer 136
washing-line 15
washing-machine 10
wasp 268
waste bin 75
waste-disposal unit 10
water 27, 77, 104, 233, **273**
water-bed 278
water bottle 278

water-butt 138
water-cooled 135
water creatures 267
water cress 145
waterfall 223, 224, 273
watering-can 15, 138, 278
water jump 206
water level 277
water rats 224
water softener 278
water tank 14, 94
water transport 243
waterworks 277
wave 173, 220, 248, 273
wavelength 291
wavy 69, 302
weary 57
weasel 263
weather 258, 294
weather-beaten 68
weather vane 259
wedding 4, 172
Wednesday 283
weed 15, 224, 271
week 280
weekend 280
weekly 294
weigh 177
weight 161, 209
weightlessness 256
weir 224, 273
weld 98
welding 115
well 32, 277
wellingtons 60
west 26
western 187, 194
wet 48, **275**
wetsuit 221
whale 267
wheat 147
wheel 232
wheelbarrow 15, 138
wheelchange 207
when 286
whirlwind 258
whisk 141
whisky 176
whisper 289
whistle 76, 195
white 69, 213
white mouse 261
white wine 176
whiting 149, 267
Whitsun 281
whooping cough 33
wicked 70
wicket 198
wicket-keeper 198
wife 1
wild creatures 263, 264
wildebeest 264
willow 270
winch 117, 244
wind 223, 254, 258
wind-cheater 58
wind gauge 259
winding gear 74
windmill 272
window 7, 92, 103
window display 177
wind pump 272
windscreen 232
wine store 176
wing 199, 250
wings 189
winner 195
winter 281
wiper 232
wire 97, 167, 240
wire basket 163
witness 108
witness-box 297
wolf 264
wood 89, 210
woods 218
wool 29, 66, 128
woollen 28
word 21
word processor 139
work 21
workshop 109
work surface 10
work top 10
worried 53
wreath 166
wreck 221
wren 265
wrench 98
wrestler 212
wrestling 212
wringing 275
wrinkled 48, 68
wrist 37
wristwatch 221
writing 19, 293

X-ray 34

yacht 220, 243, **245**
yam 145
yard 7
year 280
yeast 156
yell 289
yellow **310**
yellow lines 219
yellow pages 292
yesterday 283
yew 270
yogurt 72, 150, 155
younger 19
zebra 264
zebra-crossing 229
zero
  atmosphere 257
zero gravity 256
zinc 217
zip fastener 64